Praise for SA

"Rarely does a soul come to earth with the power to uplift the lives of countless others. Such a soul was Swami Kriyananda. Through a lifetime of service to his guru, Paramhansa Yogananda, Kriyananda was able to help people throughout the world turn their lives to God. In *Say Yes to Life!*, Nayaswami Parvati tells the story of how he personally trained her and molded her discipleship to Yogananda. It is a story of dedication, self-sacrifice, and most of all divine love."

—NAYASWAMI DEVI, spiritual director, Ananda Sangha Worldwide; author, the *Touch of Light* blog and book series

"In *Say Yes to Life!* Nayaswami Parvati tells the story of Ananda through her fifty years of leadership serving at the heart of Ananda. Working closely with Swami Kriyananda, and other core leaders, she had a front row seat to most of the seminal events that shaped Ananda's growth and transformation. Beautifully attuned to the spiritual nuances of Yogananda's and Swamiji's mission, Parvati captures the essence of Ananda's history and success."

—NAYASWAMI BHARAT (Joseph Cornell) founder, Sharing Nature Foundation; author, the *Sharing Nature* series and *AUM: The Melody of Love*

"With quiet understatement, Parvati writes of inspired spiritual adventure: miracles, world travel, and living in an old bus in the woods as well as a 45-room mansion in the city. Hers has been no ordinary life — it has been a life devoted to finding God and of service to God and Guru, guided by her spiritual teacher. Spiritual seekers will find ample inspiration in her clarity of purpose and her joyful willingness to ever and again say '*Yes!*'"

—HANSA DOSSETT Ananda minister; former technology consultant and leader

"What a story! The author's life of helping build Ananda is fascinating. Anyone curious about the development of Ananda and the dedication needed to build a spiritual work will enjoy Parvati's book."

—SUSAN USHA DERMOND, BA, MA, MLS, author, *Calm and Compassionate Children* and *Awake and Ready*; educator and administrator (retired), Living Wisdom School

"*Say Yes to Life!* is the quietly extraordinary story of a soul's journey toward Self-realization and the building of the spiritual community of Ananda. Each of these are inextricably linked.

"Unique in the telling of these stories is Nayaswami Parvati's lens and her vision: clear and undistorted by judgment, desire, or expectations. The images she conveys appear as pure color. But the deep underlying theme of this story is of attunement. This is a person's receptivity to the invaluable soul guidance offered by a spiritual teacher or guru. It has been my gift to witness attunement become manifest both vividly and profoundly in the people of Ananda.

"My heart is filled with gratitude as I read the pages of *Say Yes to Life!*, in seeing and understanding the selfless service, the love, courage, energy, humility, and joy it took, and continues to take, to build the community of Ananda."

—ANNE SCHEID Art Instructor Emerita, Fresno City College; co-leader,
Ananda Fresno Meditation Group

"Parvati, Soul Sister! We came into this incarnation less than twenty-four hours apart in time (in August 1946) and a few hundred miles in space (between Los Angeles and Sacramento). We both moved to the Bay Area in 1966 to begin our spiritual search and then to the Ananda Meditation Retreat within the same month in the summer of 1972. [*Say Yes to Life!*] does a fabulous job of describing the incredible spiritual adventure that we have shared with Swami Kriyananda and the rest of our spiritual family. It will serve as an inspiration to many!"

—NAYASWAMI NITAI director, Education for Life Foundation; author, *For Goodness Sake!*

Say Yes to Life!

Dear Rebecca,
Many blessings!
Parvati

Say Yes to Life!

*Spiritual Adventure and Discipleship
in the Building of Ananda*

Nayaswami Parvati

CRYSTAL CLARITY PUBLISHERS Commerce, California

CRYSTAL CLARITY PUBLISHERS
1123 Goodrich Blvd. | Commerce, California
crystalclarity.com | clarity@crystalclarity.com
800.424.1055

ISBN 978-1-56589-165-4 (print) | LCCN 2024009406
ISBN 978-1-56589-547-8 (e-book) | LCCN 2024009407
ISBN 978-1-56589-841-7 (audiobook)

Cover design by Tejindra Scott Tully
Interior layout and design by Michele Madhavi Molloy

 The *Joy Is Within You* symbol is registered by the Ananda Church
of Self-Realization of Nevada County, California.

Dedicated to

my guru, Paramhansa Yogananda,

my spiritual teacher, Swami Kriyananda,

and to my gurubhais, my friends in God,

who are living proof that "simplicity of living,
plus high thinking, bring the greatest happiness."

Contents

Contents

Introduction

My life with Ananda began in the summer of 1971. It was at this time that I first read *Autobiography of a Yogi*, took a meditation class series, heard about Ananda, and visited the Ananda Meditation Retreat. It was love at first sight.

I had been seeking meaning in my life for several years. I knew this meaning would need to be spiritual in nature, as I was not at all attracted to politics, social causes, or seeking wealth. When I found Ananda and Swami Kriyananda, I knew I had found what I had been looking for. I felt I had come home.

From the first time I visited Ananda, heard Swami Kriyananda speak about the spiritual teachings, and met some of the people living in the community, I felt the same vibration and consciousness that I had felt in reading *Autobiography of a Yogi*. I felt that Paramhansa Yogananda's book had found living expression in Swami Kriyananda and Ananda.

As the years have gone by, and as I have engaged deeply and regularly in meditation and the practice of Kriya Yoga, my life has become increasingly about joy. The spiritual teachings and broad scope of understanding of the meaning of life offered to me by Yogananda and Swami Kriyananda, have brought increasing understanding, expansion of awareness, and joy.

I have felt inspired, and even compelled, to write about my more than fifty years with Ananda—as a disciple, as a Kriya Yogi, and as a lover of God—to share with others the incredible spiritual adventure I have experienced in this lifetime.

It has been a life dedicated to the practice of the teachings of Self-realization, to living in a spiritual community dedicated to finding God, and to making the ongoing personal effort needed to bring about an ever-deepening experience of fulfillment and joy in God.

As the Ananda community grew, I saw that Swami Kriyananda's first priority was not about buildings but on developing individuals spiritually. He supported each of us in increasing our own energy, spiritual strength, and understanding, and invited us to be part of the creation of Ananda. He held out to us our own greatest potential, and then let us fulfill that potential in the highest way we were capable of.

There are really no words to adequately express my deep and profound gratitude to Swami Kriyananda for all that he has given me.

In divine friendship and joy,
Nayaswami Parvati

Chapter 1

Before Ananda

I began this lifetime in August of 1946 in the First Methodist Hospital in downtown Los Angeles, California. It was a wonderful time and place to come into this world!

During the same year *Autobiography of a Yogi* was first published, and for the first five and a half years of my life, Paramhansa Yogananda was living at Mt. Washington, not far from where I was growing up.

For Los Angeles, 1946 was a time of tremendous change. With the end of WWII, many of the servicemen stationed there decided to make it their home. This influx meant a scarcity of housing and jobs during the closing years of the 1940s. My parents and I moved frequently in search of both.

My grandparents, my father and two uncles, as well as a number of their friends and family from Ohio and Pennsylvania, moved to Los Angeles about 1926 (interestingly, the year of Swami Kriyananda's birth). My father graduated from Fremont High School in Los Angeles in June 1929. In October the stock market crashed; suddenly there were no jobs. For the next decade, my grandfather struggled to support his wife and three sons. For a time, he sold life insurance, but not in the ordinary way. As a member of the Masonic order, his clients were fellow Masons at Lodges all over the country. For a number of years during the Great Depression, his insurance sales work took him and his family around the country. I have photographs of their travels: at the Hoover Dam as it was being completed; in the painted desert; and in the Black Hills of South Dakota. For a year they lived in Dallas, Texas. During the building of the Golden Gate Bridge, they made the crossing to San

1

Francisco by ferry. After years of work-related travel and an experience of the America of this time, the family settled once again in Los Angeles. My father attended UCLA for several semesters in 1935–36; life seemed to be returning to normal. Then, everything changed: America entered the Second World War.

One of my uncles joined the U.S. Navy in 1940. In December 1941, while he was stationed in the Philippines aboard the USS Houston, Pearl Harbor came under attack. The following spring of 1942 his ship and several others made a run for Australia, but the timing was unfortunate. In the Sunda Strait off the island of Java, all the ships were sunk in an intense but brief battle.

All three sons served in WWII: my uncle, who was killed in action; my father, drafted in the summer of 1942; and my younger uncle, not drafted until 1945. My grandfather, also wanting to serve his country, volunteered for six years as a night watchman at Lockheed. In his late fifties, he rode a bicycle a number of miles to Lockheed and back each night.

My parents met each other in the summer of 1945. Love at first sight led to a marriage that lasted fifty-three years. I have wondered if their whirlwind romance, marriage, and my arrival soon after weren't somehow divinely arranged. Though my parents were not overtly spiritual, they had a good, clean energy that inspired trust in me as a child. They looked out for me with loving care. I never felt strange energy in our house; emotional upsets were few and far between. We were a happy family, focused on making a living, doing the best we could for ourselves, and enjoying and having fun with whatever we did have — I feel fortunate to have had them as parents. Sri Yukteswar's statement, "live within your purse," was our norm. Still, we knew how to stretch that purse to make the most of it. When we had a free day on a weekend, rather than clean house, we would often go to the beach! — not always, but often enough that life was enjoyable in the present, and never became drudgery with enjoyment only a dim possibility at some future time.

On the downside, little spirituality was expressed in our home. There was kindness, but not devotion; softness observed in other people was seen as weakness. There was a feeling that one could fully trust only one's own blood family. Those outside the family were strangers. Ours was the classic "us four and no more" syndrome described by Yogananda, and prevalent after the Great Depression and WW II. Though we did have some close friends, these friendships extended mainly to fun and social time.

Changes Begin — Going Away to College

Karma plays itself out in its own time, and so it did for me and my family. My own karma was always there, just waiting for the right time to blossom. I lived fairly happily with my parents for the first twenty years of my life. At the age of twenty, I could feel change stirring within me. The feeling came first as a growing need to get away from my family and the familiar surroundings I had grown up with. I could tell that the coming change would be an important time for me. Beginning in the fall of 1966, I spent my last two years of college at San Jose State. On every college campus, mine included, the mid-sixties were a tumultuous time. For many young people all over the country — all over the world — there was a crisis of identity and faith. I remember visiting the Haight-Ashbury in San Francisco in 1967 and thinking, "Well, it's interesting, but many of these people seem crazy to me!" I simply had too much common sense to be a hippy. I was looking for something that would give meaning to my life. But that something needed to make sense on all levels. What I wanted was not escape, but meaning. Though drugs played a small part in this exploration, I knew what I was looking for could only be found on a deeper level of understanding.

A Trip to Europe — Who Am I?

A year and a half into my time at San Jose State, now close to graduation, I realized that something was very wrong. I thought to myself, "I can't graduate yet! I don't know who I am!" I had hoped that being at college would help me know myself better. Since that hope was unfulfilled, I suddenly realized I had to begin my search for deeper meaning in earnest, and immediately! At the beginning of 1968, I decided to take off what would have been my last semester of college. A girlfriend and I decided to take a three-month trip to Europe, a journey I hoped would give me some insight and answers. My parents weren't upset with my plan; they could tell I was trying to find my way. Promising to repay my uncle and my parents, I borrowed around $600 — more than enough in that financial reality (so different from that of today) to make the trip possible.

My girlfriend and I had a great adventure as we traveled through Europe, staying with friends and relatives — a month in Greece (Athens and Corfu); a month in Spain (Barcelona and Madrid); and then on to Hanover, Germany, and Alesund, Norway. I will always be grateful for the learning experience of our travels, which helped broaden my horizons. I also came away with a much greater appreciation of the United States — of its great experiment in drawing together so many different cultures into one country. One thing that I learned early on: People are the same the world over; they have the same difficulties and successes wherever they live. Much as I enjoyed our journey, I quickly realized that travel would not give me the answers I was looking for.

As I was returning from Europe, Robert Kennedy was assassinated. Reading a news account of this in the London airport, I thought, "This feels like a good time to be going home." During our travels I had seen missiles paraded through the streets of Athens, Greece after a military takeover; I had experienced Greek Orthodox Easter on the island of Corfu. I had also spent numerous hours at the Prado Museum taking in the Goya and El Greco paintings. Arriving at the Hanover train station in northern Germany, I had felt how starkly different was the consciousness and energy there from what we had experienced in our two months in southern Europe. I had felt the frustration and cynicism of people my age caught in the class-conscious society of the Germany of that time. And I had experienced life in a small town in Norway at a time when life there was still materially simple. But in none of these experiences were there real answers to my questions about the deeper meaning of life.

The summer I returned from Europe, feeling the need for time to assimilate all I had experienced, I went to the UC Santa Barbara campus for six weeks and shared an apartment with several girls, none of whom I knew. I enjoyed not knowing anyone, simply being by myself. I rode everywhere on a bicycle, visiting the bookstore in Isla Vista frequently. It was in this bookstore that *Autobiography of a Yogi* was first pointed out to me. I remember looking at the cover and thinking, "Well, it might be interesting, but he looks like a woman, and India is so emotional." Clearly, I was not yet ready for something deeper. Nor did I know what it was I wanted. I took TM meditation initiation that summer and practiced it for a whole month! Though I sensed that meditation was a good thing, I didn't have enough clarity or focus to embrace a practice of my own. I was still looking, and thinking.

Return to College and Spirituality

When I returned to San Jose State in the fall of 1968 to complete my BA degree, who should be the scholar-in-residence but Alan Watts! Each week he gave a lecture on some aspect of the spiritual life based on his experience with Buddhism. His talks weren't deep, but were spiritually entertaining, and helped me to keep engaged at least in the *idea* of a spiritual life.

It was at this time that I met Chris Moore and began a relationship that was to last the next six years. Finding ourselves with similar spiritual interests, we began exploring these together.

From 1968 to 1970 I studied, tasted, and tested various spiritual practices and groups. I didn't actually try many of them, but did find Zen Buddhism appealing because of its simplicity and clarity. I didn't yet know about or understand devotion. I simply wasn't ready — *yet*.

By the summer of 1970, I had come to a point of desperation. Twenty-four years old, graduated from San Jose State the previous summer, I had taken a job at the local Welfare Department. I didn't find any meaning in my job and remember being horrified when my supervisor asked me to consider taking a promotion. Though I simply couldn't imagine working day after day in such an environment, I still didn't know what I did want. By this time, I wasn't at all interested in going to more spiritual meetings or groups that weren't meaningful to me. I really needed to find what was mine!

That summer I decided to quit my job by the end of the year and to use the remaining six months in the job to save as much money as I could. Although Chris and I had embarked on this new direction together, it was my energy and desperation that were the driving force. My last day of work, at the end of 1970, found me finally free to explore more fully what I was looking for.

At the beginning of 1971, Chris and I, walking by the San Jose State campus, noticed a man selling books out of his van. The book was Ram Das's recently published *Be Here Now*.

That book, coming at *that particular moment* in time, *was*, I felt, *sent to me by God*.

Finally, a chord was struck within me — the struggle he as a Westerner went through to meet his guru; his reactions to him; and ultimately, as their relationship unfolded, the devotion he felt toward him. I found all of this deeply inspiring. I could feel in Ram Das's search the nature of the path and the spiritual relationship I myself, however unknowingly, had been looking for — a solid, devotional relationship with someone who could take me deep in the spiritual life. I knew when I read this book (and it was really only the Introduction that I actually read) that I wanted to live the life he described, to leave everything and enter into it with all my heart. All that remained for me now was to discover *how*.

Finding Ananda — When the Disciple Is Ready the Guru Appears

Shortly after reading Ram Das's book, Chris and I set off, and for three months that spring we traveled. What were we looking for? A community that would support meditation and the spiritual life—a community just like Ananda! Up and down the west coast of America, from the Bay Area to Vancouver, BC, we looked for such a place. Not finding anything even close, we returned to our starting point in the San Jose area. It was here that the next cog in the wheel clicked into place.

Gazing one day at a poster advertising a six-week Yoga and Meditation class series, I thought, "Well, I'm not really that interested in yoga postures, but meditation is definitely what I'm looking for." On the way to the first class, we stopped (yet again!) at a local spiritual bookstore. My motivation was simply to find something spiritually inspiring to read. Looking at the biography section inside the front door, my eyes lit on *Autobiography of a Yogi*. I remembered the book from several years before, but at the time hadn't been interested in it. Even now my only thought was, "Well, it's big and inexpensive, and biographies are usually interesting. Let me give it a try." We went from that bookstore directly to the first of the meditation classes. When the instructor opened his briefcase, I saw that it was filled with copies of the *Autobiography*. Now my interest in reading this book definitely increased.

I read *Autobiography of a Yogi* non-stop over the next few days. I was enthralled by Yogananda: his style of writing, the way he spoke about the spiritual path, and the way he made it so accessible. The book was thrilling! And I was thrilled finally to have found something that felt like my own.

Our Yoga and Meditation Classes Begin

Our meditation class teacher was Kersee Bulsara. A student of Swami Kriyananda's, he had taken over teaching Swami's classes in the Bay Area just the year before, the year Swami had finally been able to move permanently to Ananda. Telling us about Ananda, Kersee made it sound a little difficult to actually move there—you needed to be *together*, to have *money*, and, hopefully, have some kind of *business* to support yourself. Resisting discouragement,

I thought, "Well, I'm somewhat together, we do have a little money, but I don't know much at all about business. I think I just need to go there and see it for myself." The class series ended in July; by the first weekend in August, Chris and I were on our way to visit Ananda for the first time.

First Visits to Ananda, Summer 1971

In 1971, the trip to Ananda from the Bay Area took longer than it does now. Once you left Interstate 80, the roads were not as wide and straight as they are today, especially when you left Nevada City and headed north on Hwy 49, out toward the San Juan Ridge and Ananda.

We made it to the Ananda Retreat on a Saturday afternoon.

Here is what I remember of that first visit:

First of all, as we got out of the car, the smell of kitkitdizze. Pungent and strong, this native shrub grew everywhere in the forest near the Retreat. Then as we entered the office dome, the smell of incense and fragrant oils, products of an Ananda business. Pervasive too was the heat that comes with August in the foothills of the Sierra Nevada mountains. Those first impressions remind me to this day of the Ananda Meditation Retreat.

Satya, who acted as guest master for the Retreat, was there to welcome us. Gentle and accepting, he helped us feel at home, even allowing us to camp overnight in our car so that our only expense was for our meals. Satya was there simply to welcome all who came to this place called Ananda.

After dinner that evening Swami led a satsang in the temple; accompanying himself on guitar, he played songs he had written. After the satsang, we walked through a beautiful starlit night down to our car, got settled and went to sleep. Sunday morning there was a sadhana, then breakfast, then a fire ceremony, followed by a Sunday Service given by Swami, and finally, lunch. I was thrilled simply to be there—especially to hear Swami speak about the teachings of yoga. He made the spiritual path accessible and yet full of common sense. His words had the same feeling as Yogananda's when I read *Autobiography of a Yogi*.

Tuning in to the people around Swami, I liked what I saw. They seemed to be like me: serious spiritual aspirants there to find God, and at the same time, happy and relaxed. I remember thinking, "If they can live here and do this, then so can I."

Back in Los Gatos we lived in a simple, inexpensive duplex in a country setting. I had a temporary job in the summer of 1971 as a postal carrier. Because my workday began at 6:30 am, Chris and I decided to get up at 3:30 am to do our sadhana—Energization, yoga postures, and meditation. Though we were still very new to the path, we loved our spiritual practices; especially as we began to actually experience their power.

We visited Ananda one more weekend that summer, and in the fall of 1971, we attempted to move there. I say "attempted" because our decision was quick, and not well thought out. By the end of September, the month my post office job ended, we had bought a trailer and were on our way to the Ananda Meditation Retreat. Or so we thought. The weekend we arrived was cold, rainy, and muddy—very different from the summer weather we had previously experienced, and a good reality check. A week later, it began to snow! Coming early to the Sierra mountains that year, this first storm dropped several feet of snow. I knew it was time to leave. We simply weren't prepared to winter over in a small trailer in such conditions. As it turned out, we were right to go—snow kept on coming for an exceptionally challenging winter.

In my heart, I knew I would be returning to Ananda to live. For now, what was needed was time to prepare.

Back in Los Gatos we were miraculously able to return to our same apartment. The next nine months we spent preparing to move to Ananda. We continued our spiritual practices and consciously sought to live a more spiritually focused life where we were. We kept in touch with Ananda through periodic newsletters and by subscribing to the "Dollar-a-Month" club—wonderful spiritual writings from Swami Kriyananda. And we meditated! Every day, twice a day, in preparation for our eventual return.

We practiced regularly what we had learned at Ananda—the Energization exercises, Hong Sau, and the AUM technique. A Self Realization Fellowship meditation group in nearby Los Gatos offered weekly meditations and a Sunday Service with readings, but with no speaker. Though there was no socializing, the group meetings were still a support for us. Sweet as the energy was, its effect on me was to increase my longing to be back at Ananda. I could not envision myself simply living in the city, working at a job, and practicing the teachings. I knew I needed to leave behind the life I had lived so far, and to embrace the spiritual life completely. Nothing else would do. It had to be a life totally dedicated to God. And this life had to be at Ananda and with Swami, for I now felt more deeply than ever that Ananda was my home and Swami Kriyananda my spiritual teacher.

During those nine months, I constantly felt the need to complete my preparation so that I could return to Ananda. In the spring of 1972, I knew the time was right. Chris and I readied our fifteen-foot trailer and packed our Rambler station wagon. On July 15, 1972, we set off for Ananda—our second attempt, but this time we were more fully prepared.

CYNTHIA

A poem written by my father in 1948

She's just a little girl,
Her years are only two,
With eyes of deepest blue
And hair without a curl —
Cynthia is her name.

The sun is in her hair,
Like glistening burnished gold;
Her soul is white and bold,
So child-like, fine and fair —
Cynthia is her name.

She likes to run and play
In carefree ecstacy,
And then to talk with me,
"Of things," she's wont to say —
Cynthia is her name.

It seems that time and space
And all infinity
Are there for all to see
Expressed in lasting grace —
And Cynthia is her name.

1946, My parents

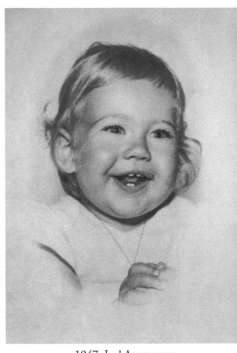

1947, Joy! At one year

1953, My grandparents

1950, Los Angeles

1957, Disneyland

Chapter 2

The Joy of Ananda

 *From the depths of slumber,*
As I ascend the spiral stairway of wakefulness,
I will whisper:
God! God! God![*]

Early Experiences of Swami Kriyananda

Reading the diaries I kept in my early years at Ananda, I remember most powerfully the *joy* I felt in being around Swami Kriyananda. Never before had I experienced such joy. It was a joy that permeated every part of Ananda. In fact, it *was* Ananda. The experience of this joy was so deep and powerful that it has remained with me to the present moment.

Swami, always a clear and deeply attuned channel for his guru, radiated this joy. No matter the challenges we encountered during the building of Ananda, whether agreeable or difficult, in his outlook and consciousness Swami always remained the same — true to Yogananda and to expressing Yogananda's teachings in every aspect of the building of Ananda. We always knew, because Swami would continually remind us, that our sole mission in this lifetime was to find God. He would also remind us that all outer circumstances, however urgent they might seem at the time, were of lesser importance. Through the many years I spent with him helping to build Ananda, I never saw Swami waver from that fundamental outlook on life. His clarity of vision and strength of purpose has allowed Ananda to navigate a straight and true course to the only goal worth pursuing in life — God alone.

[*] Lyrics from the poem "God, God, God" by Paramhansa Yogananda, in *Whispers from Eternity*. Crystal Clarity Publishers, 2008.

Something I have never forgotten are words that Swami addressed to all of us: "I saw who you were when you came [to Ananda], and I accepted you as you were." Looking at photos of us in those early years, one can appreciate a bit more just what that statement meant. We were young, untried spiritually, often opinionated, and — having lived through the 1960s — somewhat rebellious. But many of us were also sincerely seeking a deeper meaning to life, one that we'd been unable to find in "normal" society. Even if we weren't quite sure what it was all about, the spiritual path was deeply appealing to us. My eternal gratitude goes out to Swami Kriyananda for allowing me to be part of the incredible adventure called Ananda, and for being a true guide and teacher during the more than forty years I knew him.

First Years at Ananda (1972–1981)

On July 15, 1972, Chris and I arrived at the Meditation Retreat; we parked our 15-foot trailer on the present site of Happiness Lodge. And, we arrived unannounced! It's true that the lack of a telephone at the Retreat gave some validity to our not letting anyone know we were coming. But it's also true that I didn't want someone telling us (for some vague, unknown reason) that perhaps we should wait to come. And so, we simply arrived and informed Satya, the Retreat guest master, that we had come to stay. Fortunately, he also seemed to feel that our coming was a good idea!

When we visited the summer before, I had asked several people about membership. First would come a blank look, then a "yes, maybe so-and-so knows about that." I could never get any specific information. So, we actually didn't know whom to contact about moving there!

This first summer introduced us to the day-to-day reality of living at Ananda. For one thing, in July it was *hot*! At least 100 degrees the day we arrived. The Retreat was not only hot, dry, and dusty — but there was nowhere to go to cool off. No electricity, no fans, and obviously no air-conditioning. What water the Retreat had was also at a premium, and not suitable for drinking. Potable water had to be brought in from an artesian spring located at the Caughlan's in North Columbia, a few miles north on Tyler Foote Road (about four or five miles from the Retreat). To swim and cool off that summer, we often drove to the Yuba River; we actually spent a fair amount of time at the river during those first few months as we settled in to life at Ananda.

One change that struck me immediately was how many people there were to relate to! From the moment we stepped out the door of our trailer, there were so many people to greet! I believe at this time there were ninety to one-hundred people living at Ananda, including the Retreat, Ayodhya, and the Farm. Before our move, we had been living a quiet life in Los Gatos relating closely with only a few friends who shared our interest in spiritual matters. Gradually I realized that in order to live at Ananda, I needed to put out much more energy. I knew intuitively that this was just what I needed—more energy! I was now living and working in a place where people were more conscious in themselves and in their way of relating to one another than anything in my previous experience. As the days and weeks went by, and as I became more used to this new flow of energy and way of life, I began to deeply enjoy the challenges of living the spiritual life more fully.

I remember sitting outside our trailer that summer, relaxing in the shade of a tree and reading Swami's *14 Steps Lessons* (now *The Art and Science of Raja Yoga*) for the first time. Written in 1970, the lessons were offered as a correspondence course, one lesson every two weeks. They were thrilling to me—deep, inspiring, and spiritually clarifying. Even more important to me, they were practical and applicable to my everyday life! Studying these lessons in the uplifting environment of Ananda, living under the guidance of the person who had written them, I thought I had died and gone to heaven.

The Farmhouse and Ayodhya (Summer 1972)

The summer I arrived, Ananda was expanding from a main focus at the Meditation Retreat to a focus also at the Farm, and at the monastery in Ayodhya.

Upstairs in the farmhouse Seva and Jyotish managed the community's day-to-day affairs. Swami occasionally joined them there, but usually worked where he was now living, a mile and a half away, in his dome at Ayodhya. Downstairs in the Farmhouse, in what had been a living room, was the print shop for Swami's books and lessons. The presses were operated by several Farm residents; the lessons themselves were sent out by Devi. My own copy came to me literally "hot off the press"!

Clustered near Swami's dome at Ayodhya was a collection of teepees and trailers, homes of the monks and nuns who had taken vows the previous winter.

Satsang with Swami

Swami Kriyananda was very much with us in those early days. He usually gave the Sunday Service; several other ministers, Jyotish and Binay among them, did so occasionally. We were blessed with the opportunity to draw deeply and regularly from him, not only on Sundays but also in weekly satsangs at his dome at Ayodhya. (When I first met him in 1971, he was still living in the dome at the Meditation Retreat. By the summer of 1972, his new dome at Ayodhya had been completed.)

During the satsangs, Swami would talk about the spiritual life and answer questions from those present. Topics might include karma and reincarnation, the chakras, Kriya Yoga, and his separation from SRF. This time spent with him was both thrilling and essential: thrilling as a profound spiritual learning experience; essential as a catalyst for separating those in tune with Swami's vision for community (based on Yogananda's vision for World Brotherhood Colonies) from those who simply were not.

In the 1970s many people were interested in spiritual communities but had no real understanding of what they were. Swami's deeper understanding of Yogananda's vision created an energy field that drew in closer those in tune with this vision. It also helped those who were not in tune with it to find and follow their own right spiritual path. The result was an ongoing sorting-out process in the beginning years of Ananda.

Making Our Way at Ananda

Chris and I did odd jobs that summer. For a short time, I worked at the Retreat kitchen with Jamuna (Jacqueline Snitkin), who became a lifelong friend and core member of Ananda. Knowing we needed to have more full-time jobs by the fall, Chris and I were on the lookout for opportunities. The money we had brought with us would go partly for our membership fee and partly for building a house. (When we did build our house the following spring, I remember the cost being about $2,500.)

Membership

In September, a month and a half into our new life at Ananda, the membership committee finally met: Swami Kriyananda, Seva, Jyotish, Lakshmi, and several others. We approached the meeting with some concern. After all, the membership committee didn't really know us; all we had done so far was to arrive unannounced and say that we wanted to live at Ananda. But when we arrived at the meeting, everyone was relaxed and laughing. Then, with some seriousness, Swami said, "Well, should we accept them?" The others said, "Oh, I guess so." Swami then turned to us smiling and said simply: "OK, I guess you're in." And that was that! A sense of relief and happiness was there for us, as we were now accepted and could really settle in.

And so, our life at Ananda began.

Soon after we went to Seva to pay the membership fee ($1,500 for a couple). The fee itself would go to help pay off the mortgage on the land. That fall we continued living at the Meditation Retreat in our trailer. With winter coming we worked quickly to build on a small addition.

Paying work at the Farm marked a transition for us. Although we continued living at the Retreat, we now began spending more of our time at the Farm. Riding in the Retreat van, we daily commuted the twelve miles round trip to the Farm and back.

Binay had hired Chris, Keshava, Nitai and me to work making flower jewelry. We would hollow out small rounds of oak and manzanita, fill them with simple flower arrangements and clear resin, and then bake them in an old kitchen oven! After they were buffed and polished, the rounds were sold as pendants, key chains, and other items we thought people might enjoy. All through the winter of 1972–73 there was a wonderful spirit of camaraderie in our group. Nothing we did seemed odd; nothing we needed to do seemed impossible. We were just so happy to be living at Ananda!

Ananda had little outward structure at this time; its unfoldment was organic and fluid. The people living there weren't told what to do. Rather they were inspired to offer their energy freely. When there was a real need, somehow help would arrive — people would show up and deal with the challenge — a tree across the road, a car stuck in a ditch, deer in the garden. Those who stepped forward to help most willingly were especially those who were drawing spiritually from Swami. Those who wanted to grow spiritually and deepen their discipleship to Yogananda followed his lead. Acting spontaneously in response to people's need was Swami's living example. He set the tone for the entire unfolding community.

Tuning in to Swami

Although difficult to describe, the feeling of the living reality of these early years was palpable. Those who understood what Swami, as a direct disciple of Yogananda, had to offer, stayed close to him and "included themselves." They are the ones who became part of the core energy of Ananda; they drew from Swami as much as they possibly could. Even when he wasn't physically present, we kept a strong sadhana and meditated together frequently. I clearly remember thinking at the time that the most important things I had to do in my life at Ananda were to tune in to Swami's energy and consciousness, and to meditate.

I took advantage of every opportunity to be with him — teas, Sunday Services, classes, Kriya initiations, and any satsangs or meetings in which he was present. I could feel that the purpose of any time with Swami was to learn, certainly, but even more to attune to his vibration and consciousness. I thought at the time, "For me, Swami is Yogananda's representative in a physical body; that is how I will relate to him." Swami made it clear, and I myself understood, that he wasn't the guru; but at the same time, I felt strongly that relating to Swami as Yogananda's representative would help me grow spiritually. I needed to have a way to do this.

Daily Life at the Farm

For many of those living at the Farm, life was not easy. To help people, Jyotish, serving as community manager, lived there and sought to help people spiritually and in many other ways. The vibration at the Farm itself was more mixed than at the Meditation Retreat or at Ayodhya. Both families and single people lived at the Farm; many were struggling both spiritually and financially. Within this diverse mix of people and attitudes, there were naturally conflicting cross currents of energy and ideas about what this newly evolving spiritual community should be. I was often surprised that within this group quite a few were simply not interested in drawing this understanding from Swami.

The physical plane brought its own challenges — roads that alternated between dirt and mud; a primitive water system; limited access to electricity and phone; heat from wood gathered in the forest or from 25-gallon propane cylinders. Without its own temple, the Farm had no structured, daily sadhana. The Retreat, six miles away, did offer regular sadhanas, but was not an option for most people. Even with these constraints, those of us strongly enough motivated did find ways to meditate together regularly. We meditated upstairs in the Farmhouse, in people's homes, and even in the fields. Inspired by this new spiritual life together, and by Swami's living example, we made the effort to support one another in keeping our sadhana regular and strong.

First Winter at Ananda: Swami Travels to India

During my first winter at Ananda, Swami was finally able to make a long-awaited return visit to India. A number of those who had traveled down from Ananda to see him off at the San Francisco airport gathered first at his parents' home in Atherton for a farewell satsang. It was here that I met his parents for the first time.

For the preceding ten years Swami had been unable to get a visa to visit India. Someone had reported him to the Indian government as a Christian missionary. This blow fell soon after he was called back from India and summarily dismissed from Self-Realization Fellowship — thus cutting Swami off both from his guru's organization in the United States and from India, his spiritual home. The visa situation was finally resolved in 1972. Swami's visit to India lasted three months, and included visits to Ananda Moyi Ma, Swami Muktananda, Satya Sai Baba, and Swami Narayan, all movingly described in his book *Visits to Saints of India*.

Swami's trip to India took place only a few months after I had arrived at Ananda and extended through Christmas and Master's birthday celebrations. Since I was still getting used to living in a very new and different environment, his absence didn't affect me as much as one might imagine. I knew I had found my spiritual home at last; now I simply needed time to adjust to this wonderful new life. It wasn't only the social and spiritual environments that were new. I was also adjusting to living in the foothills of the Sierra mountains — rain (sixty inches per year); snow (two to four feet several times in the winter); propane heating (learning how to hook up and operate individual propane tanks); and kerosene and propane lamps and refrigerators. The nearest laundromat was fifteen miles away in Nevada City. We happily compared notes with each other on which propane lamps gave the best lighting; which caulking worked best for hooking up those indispensable propane tanks; and, for those with wood stoves, how to keep wood dry during the long, cold, wet winters. Among kerosene lamps the Aladdin was considered the best. As you can imagine, dealing with all of this took up a fair amount of our time—and energy!

While Swami was away that first winter people went through transitions: Several left the community; some monastics left the monastery; and several couples split up while other new couples formed. Swami knew that such changes were inevitable, and, in his wisdom, let them play themselves out. He knew people would grow from these experiences, and they certainly did.

At the time, I was too new at Ananda to understand, or to even be interested in these changes. Because I had arrived at Ananda only a few months earlier, I didn't know most of the people involved that well. My focus was on dealing with my own new life—the physical plane, regular meditations, my own spiritual life in general, and work. Although I could sense that these changes made the community seem a bit unsettled, I could also feel that the basic energy at Ananda was holding together. Swami had established a core energy at the Meditation Retreat and at Ayodhya; that core energy continued unabated in his absence. Sunday Services continued at the Retreat, as well as regular group meals, sadhanas and meditations. When Swami did finally return from his trip, we were very happy to have him back with us and to again be giving Sunday Services as well as satsangs and teas at his dome.

My Parents Visit!

In December 1972, just after a heavy snowfall, my parents suddenly appeared outside our trailer! Concerned about my new and strange (to their way of thinking) lifestyle, and wanting to see if I was all right, they had driven to Nevada City, rented chains, and driven out on the snow-covered roads to find Ananda. Somehow, they had managed to make it to the bottom of the Meditation Retreat hill, then parked and walked through the snow up the Retreat road to find me. I was absolutely amazed! Nice as it was to see them, to this day I do not understand how they, accustomed to paved city streets and signs, were able even to find the Retreat road, and then to continue driving for two and a half miles through the snow on a remote gravel roadway! After that memorable first visit, they continued to drive up to see me from their home in the Bay Area (under much better conditions!) three or four times a year. After all, I was their only child and they simply needed to see me periodically.

I don't think my parents ever really understood the spiritual reasons motivating me to live at Ananda. What they did understand, and what helped them to accept my new way of life, was the people they met there. And, most importantly, they saw that I was happy.

Master's Market Begins (Spring 1973)

From my diary at that time:

March 24, 1973, Saturday—Today we began cleaning out the small room in the Farmhouse which is soon to become a store. It was nice to be working there.

April 16, 1973, Monday—The first day of my new store! It is truly a needed thing and a good place to put my energy.

April 20, 1973, Good Friday—A beautiful windy day today. I worked at Binay's (making jewelry) and had the store open this morning. We certainly have many good opportunities to work out karma here and also to learn wonderful new ways of behaving.

During my first winter at Ananda, and especially when I began working at the Farm, I became aware that people living there had nowhere to buy food. The closest small store, six miles away in North San Juan, didn't offer much in the way of healthy food. There was a gas station there, three bars, and Toki's restaurant (which did serve a good Yaki Soba noodle dish). Nevada City was fifteen miles away, much too far to go for many of the Farm residents, when not everyone had a car. During that winter a number of people had begun buying food from the Retreat kitchen, but doing this was not sustainable. Asha, then in charge of the kitchen, simply couldn't keep up with the demand.

Since I was now at the Farm each day, I saw firsthand the need for a way to provide basic foods such as fruits and nuts. Though my initial thought was of a few boxes of these items, the needs of the time quickly propelled things forward to a greatly expanded inventory!

In almost every satsang Swami emphasized, "If you see something that needs to be done here, then do it!" We were the ones, he was telling us, who were going to make this community a reality. Through his own example of dynamic energy and magnetism, Swami showed us how to use the principles that Master had given us. Developing Master's Market, I had the wonderful opportunity to put these principles into practice.

Though I had no money to start this project, I don't remember thinking of this as much of an obstacle. My thought was that I could manage to buy at least a couple of boxes of fruit each month to get things started. Although my own understanding of how the market would develop was limited, I found Divine Mother was there helping me each step of the way.

At first Master's Market occupied the tiny room presently serving as the Market office. Here, during lunch time, I opened for business — selling bananas and oranges, nuts, and dates, expanding to other needed items as space allowed. To support myself, I continued working mornings making flower jewelry.

A few months into the project, a young man showed up who was not only interested in making the Market a reality but was ready to put in the amazing amount of $500. Sanjaya (Jerry Whelan) helped me transform the few boxes of food I was selling into a working Market. We were now able to expand quickly into several additional downstairs rooms of the farmhouse.

Shelving went up; many more food items arrived. Bookkeeping and paperwork I handled in the office on the second floor of the

Farmhouse. To protect the produce case and a newly acquired ice cream freezer, we enclosed the Market porch in plastic over the winter. Master's Market, the name we gave the store at that time, soon became a hub of Farm life—a place not only for buying food but also for connecting with one another, an even greater need for Ananda residents at that time.

From the beginning, I saw the Market as a community center and a spiritual service. To help the Market continue, Sanjaya and I kept our salaries on a subsistence level, putting any profit back into the business. It was important to us to contribute to the upkeep of the Farm by paying our community fees; but beyond this, our actual take-home income was the small amount needed for food and utilities. Simple living and high thinking, as Yogananda had said, brings the greatest happiness. We had the wonderful opportunity to experience this principle directly. During these years, I spent a lot of time meditating and much of the rest of my time working at the Market. Through serving in this way, I could feel I was gaining a deeper understanding of how to balance service and meditation, of how to live the spiritual life on a daily basis.

The Market constantly sought new ways to serve community residents—a deli with prepared food for lunches; an outlet for Ananda's dairy and garden; movies on the lawn as a way to raise funds for an Ananda School movie projector; crates of fruit brought up from the Sacramento valley for canning; and a way for people to order foods in bulk.

Perhaps the greatest service Master's Market provided was in helping Ananda members feel that the community itself was, little by little, becoming a reality.

Swami's Leadership Style: Individual Responsibility and the Need for Balance

In this early time at Ananda, I very much appreciated Swami's leadership style: he gave us his energy, support, inspiration, and the freedom to be creative; at the same time, he made it clear that we were *responsible for ourselves*. We were, each one, responsible for supporting ourselves, buying our own food and clothing, paying fees for maintenance and utilities, and providing our own housing.

Swami's emphasis on personal responsibility meant that Ananda was not a *commune*, but a *community*. This distinction made sense to me, and provided me and many others a sense of normalcy and a grounding connection to the world we had left. We had our own money and could keep it; we could buy the food we wanted; we had a personal life of our own, *and* were part of a community. Living at Ananda meant finding a balance between what we shared as a community and what was unique to each of us as an individual.

Swami emphasized the need for the same balance in our meditation practice. Group meditations, he said, were important for getting our energy moving, but could not take the place of our personal spiritual efforts. From Swami and from one another we received tremendous support; with that support as a foundation, we knew each one of us needed to make our own spiritual effort if we were to progress. As Master said, "You must each individually make love to God." Union with God is not found as a group, but through personal effort. Swami captured this essential principle in what was for many years the theme song for Ananda: *Go On Alone* (later titled, *Walk Like a Man*). We all laughed at the irony of the title, but it did exemplify the spirit of Ananda in those days. Drawing on the support of our gurubhais, *and* being dynamically alone with God—always the essential, underlying balance for this community called Ananda.

The Publications Building —
Symbol of Ananda's Future

In the spring of 1973, the print shop and all other offices located in the Farmhouse—publications, correspondence, and community offices—moved up the hill to the newly completed Publications building (now Hansa Temple). When Swami first proposed the

Publications building, he received strong opposition from a group of Farm residents. They wanted the Farm to remain rustic—to continue to have the back-to-the-land feel so popular in the seventies. This group saw no need for a building for outreach. Swami saw Ananda as something to share with the world; this group saw the community as for the residents. Those opposed to outreach were also overlooking the simple fact that it was Swami who had worked to buy the land and who was continuing to work to pay off the mortgage.

The Publications building held great significance for me. I had seen the concrete slab for its foundation in 1971 during my first visit. The main construction took place during the months before I moved to Ananda. By the summer of 1972 the building was nearing completion and was finished in the spring of 1973.

This building itself was a physical symbol of the future of Ananda. The first new public building built at the Farm, its completion showed us what was possible for the time ahead. When I first entered the finished building, my thought was, "Thank God, Swami built this building!" The space was clean, had a beautiful view, and gave us hope that Ananda could move forward. The building gave form to Swami's maturing vision for a world brotherhood colony, expressing a dynamic balance between a spiritual lifestyle and an expansive sharing of that lifestyle with the world. All of those who had worked with Swami, who had given their energy and support, felt they had played an essential role in bringing his vision into physical form. Most of those who had worked at the Farmhouse—among them Jyotish, Seva, Asha, Lakshmi, and Devi—now had offices in the front of the new building; in back was the print shop.

With the completion of the Publications building, I felt Swami had put his stamp on the Farm. The original Farmhouse, where I worked every day, was old, leaky and a bit depressing. The Publications building, looking out from the hillside, gave concrete form to Swami's vision for the future of Ananda. It wasn't perfect; it didn't even have central heating or indoor bathrooms, but it was new, clean and dry, inspiring, beautiful.

This building also stood in marked contrast to the other deteriorating farm structures and rustic dwellings of the residents. It's helpful to remember that at this time most people at Ananda lived *very* simply—small, rustic houses, domes, teepees, trailers, buses, plastic A-frames, and tree houses, most with no electricity or running water. Looking out over the Farm from its hilltop, the new building represented a dramatic upsurge in energy and inspiration for all of us—hope for a better community, hope for a better world.

A Move to Separate

During Swami's absence the winter of 1972–73, a group living at the Farm tried to establish a Farm Council that would separate the Farm from the Meditation Retreat and Ayodhya. Their goal was to remove the Farm from Swami's control. The main energy behind this movement came from a man named Jim. One council meeting I attended became so contentious by the end that some people were weeping. When Swami returned from India, he took a firm stand for a united Ananda. Insisting that he did not want a spirit of separation, he created a Village Council that included all three areas—the Meditation Retreat, the Farm, and Ayodhya—with council representatives from each area. The Farm from then on began to feel more part of Ananda; Swami's vision for the community embraced all three areas. Jim and his family left Ananda soon after this but remained living in the area for some time.

Swami was at this time humbly feeling his way in understanding his role at Ananda. I remember an exchange in the Common Dome at the Meditation Retreat. Speaking with Asha, Seva and myself, Swami asked if we thought that he should say that he was the spiritual leader of the community. A number of us did see him in this way; a number of others did not share this view. To me, who clearly saw Swami as Ananda's spiritual leader, it seemed odd that he would ask such a question. The real question he was asking was how to be the spiritual leader of Ananda without seeming authoritarian. Those who did not relate to Swami as the spiritual guide for the community were sensitive about — and strongly opposed to — anything that felt like top-down direction. The members of this group, unsurprisingly, and over the coming years, little by little moved away from Ananda.

We Build a House at the Farm!
(Spring and Summer 1973)

Working without electricity, and with only rudimentary knowledge of construction, Chris and I, along with several friends, did much of the work with hand tools and rough-cut lumber from local sawmills — Sage's and Treloar's. Siting our house in the area called Parcel A (at the top of Ayodhya Way and up the hill above the water tank), we got approval for our house plans from the Nevada City Health Department and began to build. Paneling the interior walls with locally available pecky cedar, buying roofing and other needed materials in town, we began building in May and moved in later that summer.

I must say that the end product was a joy to live in — two lofts, a dormer window, and a deck with wonderful views of the forest and distant mountains. (This house burned to the ground in the fire of 1976 — actually a good outcome, for like most houses at the Farm, ours was most definitely *not* built to code and would eventually have been officially condemned by the local county planning department.)

But for the time being, I was very happy to be living close to nature. I loved the simplicity of our life, the quiet, the space around the house that allowed me to enjoy the sounds and fragrances of the surrounding forest. Walking everywhere, as we often did in those early years, intensified my awareness of the natural rhythms and beauty of the forest we were living in.

My love of simplicity was a blessing. Without electricity, we used propane for heat, lighting, and a refrigerator (a true luxury!). Without running water, we hauled what we needed for drinking and cooking up the hill in a truck. Instead of a bathroom, we had an outhouse; for bathing, we walked to the small shower house down at the Farm.

For me, it was a lovely time to be living at the Farm — I was deeply engaged in the spiritual life, was within walking distance of Ayodhya and Swami's dome, and was happily working at Master's Market: home, work, and spiritual life, one harmonious whole.

I Receive a Spiritual Name

It was on May 11, 1973, that I received the spiritual name of Parvati. (I had requested a name from Swami some months earlier.) Seeing me in the back of the farmhouse that day (the breezeway, as we called it then), he simply said to me, "I think your name should be Parvati." The name immediately felt right. It was a blessing then and has continued to be so to the present time.

That same morning, I attended my first Ananda wedding. It was for Jaya and Sadhana Devi Helin, two founding members of Ananda. Swami officiated as we gathered for the ceremony at their newly built house at the Farm.

I myself loved living at the Farm during those first years. I loved the freedom it gave to explore the spiritual life on my own. There was beauty everywhere on the land, especially in the springtime. Wildflowers were everywhere. I felt close to nature, and in tune with nature's rhythms.

Living at the Farm still presented challenges for someone who, as was true of me, wanted to follow Swami's spiritual leadership. The back-to-the-land energy of many of the residents in those early days, their resistance to Swami's leadership, the lack of a Farm temple and of regular sadhanas or group meditations was strong. But all these obstacles were more than offset by the presence at the Farm of many great souls, dynamic and deeply committed to Swami and his vision for Ananda: Jyotish held the fort as community manager; Jaya and Sadhana Devi and their baby Shyama were living in their newly built house; Lakshmi lived there with Gyandevi, born the

summer of 1973; Nitai was developing the school; Shivani and
Arati worked in the garden; and Nakula and Gomata ran the dairy.

The Spirit of Ananda

My experience of the spirit of Ananda in these early years was
twofold: personal, in love for God and dedication to the spiritual
life, and at the same time impersonal—detached from this world.
Swami himself was more impersonal in those days. A number of us
living at the Farm meditated together often—in the mornings, at
noon, and in the evenings, and frequently for a three-hour meditation on Saturday night. It was especially during those shared meditations that I felt the personal/impersonal spirit of Ananda.

In the years before the fire of 1976, I often felt we were living between two worlds—the material and the spiritual—with
only a thin veil separating them. We lived mostly without electricity, running water, telephones, or television. Having few cars,
we walked everywhere. Only occasionally would we make a trip
to town. Without the usual worldly influences, it was even more
apparent and deeply felt that we were living in a forest ashram,
guided by a direct disciple of a great master. It was a truly amazing
time. In 1975, to a group of us Swami said: "Remember, these are
the golden years."

For many of us this was a magical time—an experience of the
spiritual life of ancient India translated to our village in the foothills of twentieth-century California.

Even so, following Swami Kriyananda's example, we were
down-to-earth and practical in dealing with the immediate
challenges that we faced as we built Ananda. It was a time filled
with many opportunities to practice living between two worlds.

Early Miracles

We lived in a world of miracles—coming so frequently and
feeling so familiar that we accepted them as perfectly natural. Seva's

face, badly burned by exploding gasoline, healed completely without pain, the scarring all but invisible. Kalyani caught her hair on the jewelry buffer and broke her neck; her recovery was complete. Santosh, driving a truck towing a large trailer, lost control when the brakes failed on the downhill grade toward the Yuba River. Just as the truck went over the edge of the road onto the sheer drop to the river below, the trailer caught on a tree and held. The man riding in the passenger seat, not himself part of Ananda, was so affected by the experience that from that time on he faithfully shopped at Master's Market. Vijay, after falling sixty feet out of a tree, used a cane for a time, then was perfectly fine. A woman working on a construction project fell several feet onto a six foot metal stake. The steel rod miraculously missed major arteries and organs; the wound healed without the often-fatal infection common to such injuries. The doctor at the hospital was, to say the least, impressed.

And these are just a few of the miracles that I remember from those early days.

Swami's Vision for Ananda

Swami knew where Ananda was headed. He wanted us to be channels for Master's consciousness into the world, serving the many people who would come to us, thirsty for Truth and a deeper meaning to life. A series of events—the fire in 1976, publication of *The Path* in 1977,[†] and the Joy Tours in 1978—lifted us from seeing ourselves narrowly as an isolated ashram in the foothills to seeing ourselves as Swami saw us: channels for Master's mission in the world. Swami led the way, his vision of the future of Ananda evolving, broadening as his own understanding deepened. As Swami expanded, so did those of us who were in tune with him.

The Joy Tours brought a new phase of Ananda's expansion: The wonderful souls Swami met on the tours began to arrive. These enthusiastic, inspired new arrivals helped us not only rebuild the

[†] Swami Kriyananda edited this title, and reissued it later as *The New Path: My Life with Paramhansa Yogananda*. Crystal Clarity Publishers, 2009.

community, but also become more dynamic channels for Master's mission in this world. It was at this time too that we started the Earth Song Café and Market and the Mountain Song clothing and boutique store in Nevada City, both acting as a service to the broader community and as a means of spiritual outreach.

During this time of dynamic change and growth I could feel the community already established 'in spirit,' even though the outward physical buildings and infrastructure were not yet present. A feeling of deep love, power, and upliftment permeated the land—Ananda's spirit most beautifully expressed in the upward and outward soaring architecture of the Publications building. At a time when further construction of public buildings wasn't feasible, this building served as a beacon of Ananda's light, sending books, lessons, recorded talks, and correspondence to truth-seeking souls all over the world.

The Path: Swami's Life of Discipleship

When I first read *The Path*, shortly after Swami completed the writing, I felt myself living the life with Yogananda that Swami described. Yogananda's spirit and consciousness flowed strongly through Swami. Never did he in any way put himself forward as the guru. Always Swami was completely himself. Many who came to Ananda in those early years came with joy, love, and devotion. For those whose primary goal was to immerse themselves in Yogananda's path, Swami was there for them as a true teacher and guide. He introduced us to Master, especially to his energy and consciousness, and helped us understand how to attune ourselves to him. He never placed himself between us and Master, but always put himself in the role of loving disciple. Seeing how he lived his life showed us how it would be to live with Master. Watching him, I learned how to feel and live the teachings.

I saw Swami as loving and impersonal (with no conflict between the two qualities)—vigorous, dynamic, powerful, and joyful. Though it wasn't always easy to be around his high level of energy,

I found myself magnetically drawn to it. I knew that if I wanted to grow on this path, it was essential for me to be in Swami's presence, to draw on his energy and consciousness. Where some saw Swami acting from ego, even overbearing, what I saw was that he simply had more energy than most people had ever experienced — so much so that people, unable to meet him on such a high level, felt overwhelmed. Those of us who related to him as teacher and guide were deeply grateful that, while remaining impersonal, he shared his whole life with us. He was open, generous, and loving, and available to us for inspiration, guidance, and support. Swami made his spiritual life accessible to us; the life he lived as a disciple of Yogananda, he shared with us in great love, openness, and joy. Always his purpose was to help us also to live in the deep joy of discipleship to Yogananda.

I cannot say too strongly that the feeling of Ananda for me, and for many who came here, was one of great joy — the joy of living the spiritual path fully and completely, immersed in Yogananda's teachings every day, experiencing first-hand how alive and applicable to all areas of life they are. This joy is at the heart of Ananda — it is the heart of Ananda. It is this joy that makes Ananda such a strong spiritual magnet for Yogananda's spirit to this day. Experiencing Swami's energy and consciousness showed us that it was possible to live such a life completely, not only as individuals, but as a community that both supports and expresses the same joyful life.

Swami's Life of Service

Sunday mornings at the Meditation Retreat Swami would perform a fire ceremony at 10:00 am, then a break, then Sunday Service at 11:00 am, followed by lunch together in the Common Dome. Afterward, he often would give interviews to the many people (mainly from outside the community) who had come to see him. Sunday Services were open to the public; not surprisingly many more people attended when Swami gave the talk. From the beginning of Ananda, the Retreat provided a way for us to reach outside the community to the wider world. It was this outreach that kept the Ananda community from becoming isolated. The Retreat's broader purpose was that it also gave us a way to serve others. In those early years, Swami himself did most of the serving! He was at the center of almost every form of outreach. The rest of us helped as best we could, but these years were clearly a time for absorbing Swami's energy and following, to the best of our ability, where he led.

The scope of Swami's service was breathtaking. Not only was he building a community and giving many of the Sunday Services and Retreat classes, but he was also travelling as a public lecturer. His public role sometimes took him away from the community to attend spiritual events in the US and Europe. In order to keep the community growing and our outreach expanding, he would meet with key people in each area—including publications, the Retreat, and the schools—to help focus and energize their development. As an example, in the early 1980s, he gave an entire weekend program on Education for Life and the principles that define it. We watched in awe as again and again Swami set aside planned personal time to respond to community needs or calls to public service outside Ananda. While he did try to take time for himself, many times his busy schedule or the needs of the community would take precedence.

Swami at Ayodhya

Especially precious to us were teas hosted by Swami in his dome—usually late afternoon on Sundays but sometimes during the week as well. Though we had no telephones, word-of-mouth brought a quick response from those fortunate enough to hear. Not everyone in the community could attend a tea at one time—there simply wasn't room in his dome. Although usually a good-sized group came for the satsang and for the simple joy of being with Swami, there was a special sweetness in the teas when only a few were gathered. Swami would serve us Earl Grey tea in china cups—a little refinement in the midst of our daily struggles with life on the material plane. It was especially refreshing to sit in a real house, to enjoy its uplifting vibration and beautiful view. Though Swami, like the rest of us, had very little materially, whatever he did have, he freely shared with us, his spiritual family.

Swami would sit in a rocking chair; those who had come would fill the room, perhaps forty or more sitting wherever we could—couch, chairs, floor. The sheer weight of so many people packed into a structure perched on a steep hillside and supported only by four-by-four posts gave Swami some concern—always expressed lightly and humorously—that the dome might one day simply topple over and slide down the hillside. Subsequent work years later on the footings, where the four-by-four posts had become disconnected to those footings, made it clear how right Swami's intuition had been—another miracle in a community history already filled with many instances of divine protection and grace.

Conversation at these teas covered a variety of topics: Swami would answer questions about the spiritual path, the life of a devotee, his vision for Ananda, whatever were the questions or concerns voiced. He could in this informal setting share the teachings in ways deeply personal to each of us. He spoke also about his own life, his separation from SRF, and about his time in India. Each satsang was unique—the questions asked, Swami's answers, and how open he felt he could be in his answers, all depended on who was there.

Swami as Community Leader

Because Swami now lived near the Farm, he would sometimes come into Master's Market. It was wonderful to have him walk in, perhaps to buy milk from the dairy and produce from the garden. In his presence we felt him personally giving his energy and support to what we were doing.

Swami's support was always on an energetic level—it was not his way to intrude himself into the day-to-day details of store management. His way of relating to the Market throws light on the often-asked question: How are decisions made at Ananda? Following Swami's example and guidance, we have always kept decision making and management at the grassroots level, as close as possible to the work being done. The broader the impact of any decision, the more people are included in the decision-making process. We want to be sure that the concerns of everyone affected are taken into account.

When I started the Market, Swami gave me no direct instructions, nor did he ever ask how we were doing financially. Here as elsewhere he focused on the energy of the project; by feeling the energy, he could tell if it was going in the right direction. His way of leading was to inspire us and energize us spiritually, then to encourage us to use our natural creativity to find the best ways to carry our service forward.

As a leader, he excelled at drawing out people's full potential—at bringing their creativity and confidence to the fore. His way of working with people created a sweet and deep feeling of spiritual family among us, a family of which he was clearly the head—and the spiritual center. Anyone who wanted to dive deep into this path drew from him. A true swami and a deeply attuned direct disciple of Yogananda, he radiated to all who were in tune Master's power and grace; he supported us in our service, and in our spiritual lives, always putting our individual spiritual welfare ahead of any pragmatic consideration.

As I reflect on those days, I can see how Swami worked with our energy. He helped us understand the teachings, *by doing*, by experiencing directly how to get our energy moving and how to direct it once it was moving. He also helped us understand how to magnetize what we were doing so that our service was attuned to Master and his path. Then, he gave us the freedom to experiment in whatever way called us, whether in starting a business or creating a school—always with a spirit of adventure, and as an opportunity to use the principles of yoga brought to us by Master in his multi-faceted teachings.

The Gardens at Ananda

The gardens were a world unto themselves. Haanel Cassidy, who directed the work in the Ananda gardens, brought with him a wealth of knowledge about bio-dynamic gardening. Each morning, he would drive in his small pickup truck from his home at the Meditation Retreat, carefully timing his commute to arrive at the Farm at 7:00 am sharp. Those working with Haanel found themselves in an advanced, hands-on gardening class. Shivani, Ananta, and Maria worked with Haanel full time for many years; Seva served occasionally in the garden until she was needed in the office. Anandi, Devi, and Arati also gardened part time until Swami enlisted them in Ananda's outreach, both in the Publications building and at the Ananda Meditation Retreat. For some, the garden became a way of life. Their service allowed garden produce to be sold at Master's Market. The garden crew also looked after the two dwarf apple tree orchards at the Farm, one by the road and one by the school. Because in those early years there was not enough manpower to care for them more carefully, the harvest from them came only every other year. Even so, when the orchards did produce, it was a bumper crop! Grateful for the abundance, we dried, canned, and experimented creatively with what we had been given.

Music at Ananda

From the first time I visited Ananda in 1971, music was always a strong presence. In the early days, Swami provided most of the music himself. At one Saturday evening satsang at the Meditation Retreat, he played the guitar and sang the song "Little Kathy." I didn't know what to think of it. I had already left behind the rajasic psychedelic music of the 1960s; before Ananda I listened more to Joan Baez and other folk singers. But *Little Kathy*? It was a stretch for me to appreciate it. But deeper than my reaction, I could feel the innocence of the song—its heart-softening quality. Softening the heart was, I knew, important spiritually. I understood that it was devotion that had been missing from my own life and from every spiritual tradition I had experienced so far. The other songs I remember hearing during these early years — *What is Love?*, *Brothers, Come Gather Round*, *Walk Like a Man*, *If You're Seeking Freedom*, and *Peace* — all reinforced my growing recognition of devotion as essential to the spiritual life.

Swami was doing more than simply creating his own music. An accomplished singer, he also shared with us deeply devotional Bengali bhajans — songs to God from India's deepest spiritual traditions. When Swami lived in India (1958–61), he had the opportunity to sing the bhajans for Ananda Moyi Ma, among them "Emon dine ki hobe Ma Tara" (Will That Day Come to Me, Ma), "Gokula Chandra" (*Moon of Gokula*), and "Amara shad na mithilo" (O Mother, my earthly dreams have all fled away).

In addition, Swami wrote music just for fun! In one burst of creative energy, he wrote music for eighteen songs whose lyrics appear in Shakespeare's plays. It was great fun to sing them: *Who is Sylvia?*; *Hark, Hark the Lark*; *Full Fathom Five*; *Come Away Death*; *Blow Thou Winter Wind*; *All that Glisters*; *Desdemona's Song*; *Fairies' Lullaby*; *Fairies' Song*; *Imogen's Song*; *The God's Blessing*; *It Was a Lover and His Lass*; *O Mistress Mine*; *Under the Greenwood Tree*; *Where is Fancy Bred?*; *Where the Bee Sucks*; *Spring Song*; *When I Was a Boy*.

Swami Kriyananda went on to write nearly 400 pieces of music, including the *Christ Lives Oratorio*, the *Egyptian Suite*, the *Ananda Wedding* music, the Festival of Light music, music for births and deaths, music to welcome and to say goodbye, music to bless food and to bless people. Honoring many different occasions, Ananda people would break out in song. Later in his life, Swami remarked, "It sometimes feels as though we are living in an operetta here at Ananda!"

A Second Trip to India (1974)

In the spring of 1974, Swami traveled again to India, taking with him Jyotish, Nalini, Shraddha, and John Messina. They first visited Master's shrines in Calcutta. When they went on to Delhi,

Swami visited friends from his 1958–62 stay, including Rani Bhan, and her son Indu. Rani had been instrumental in helping Swami with the ill-fated Delhi project. It was she who had made possible the interview with Jawaharlal Nehru that led to Nehru's giving approval for the project.

The group also attended a satsang with Ananda Moyi Ma and were blessed to have a private audience with her. Jyotish had brought several rudraksha malas with him, and at his request Ma blessed them. He also meditated with them at Lahiri Mahasaya's house in Varanasi and at Sri Yukteswar's ashram in Serampore. On his return, he gave these beads to many of us living at Ananda. As we received them, it made us feel we had made the journey with them — feeling the deep spiritual vibrations of their pilgrimage, and especially of their visit with Ananda Moyi Ma. Through them, we felt a special connection with India. At the time, I felt the mundane, material world separating us hardly at all from the deep spiritual realm this group had brought back to us.

Spiritual Teachers Visit Ananda

During these early years a number of spiritual teachers visited Ananda and brought their blessings as well as their curiosity. I think it was interesting for the Indian swamis who visited to see how a spiritual community was faring in America. We found it a special treat to have them visit us. The satsangs with these visitors were held in the temple at the Meditation Retreat, usually followed by a meal.

Those who blessed Ananda with their presence included Swami Chidananda (President of Divine Life Society, Rishikesh) in 1970; Swami Satchidananda who visited several times in the 1970s; Roy Eugene Davis visited several times; Adano Ley (a direct disciple of Master's) visited from Canada. Other prominent swamis and teachers who visited included Swami Nadabrahmananda, Swami Venkateshananda, Swami Hridayananda, and Sant Keshavadas. The first three were direct disciples of Swami Sivananda. Nadabrahmananda was a master of Indian music as well as a swami.

During his satsang, he placed a coin on the top of his head, and made it vibrate and move by chanting AUM. Swami Hridayananda (a woman) had been Sivananda's medical doctor during his lifetime; and Swami Venkateshananda had been Sivananda's secretary. Sant Keshavadas visited several times with his wife, sharing with us through chanting and storytelling.

There were also a few teachers who came looking for disciples—inappropriate behavior for someone visiting the ashram of another spiritual teacher, all the more so when the ashram leader was absent. Swami's response was to suggest that we invite other teachers less frequently, and not at all when he wasn't there.

Swami Venkateshananda and the 1977 India Faire

A wonderful exception to Swami's caution was Swami Venkateshananda. I was inspired by this swami: A true representative of the real spirituality of India, and a shining example of someone showing deep respect for another spiritual teacher and path while maintaining his own dignity. In his early years on the path, Venkateshananda had been close to Sivananda while serving as Swami Sivananda's secretary. Even though Swami Kriyananda would be in seclusion in India, he gave his blessing to our inviting Venkateshananda to come for our India Faire in the summer of 1977. At the Faire, Venkateshananda (who had a work in Canada, as well as an ashram on the island of Mauritius, in the Indian Ocean east of Madagascar) spoke eloquently and with deep respect about Yogananda and Swami Kriyananda.

In his own newsletter, Swami Venkateshananda wrote about his visit to Ananda that summer:

"The sylvan heights of the Sierra Nevada mountains had once attracted the Gold Rush and all its subsequent tragicomedy. A rush for gold has left many scars in the glorious mountains; today there is a rush for God, but this is constructive, purifying, soul-uplifting, and healing. Several spiritual communities have sprung up in that area and are strengthening the spiritual vibrations there.

"One that is of special importance and significance is what is known as the Ananda Farm or the Ananda Meditation Retreat. This is where Life meets the Divine and the Divine Life is born.

"Ananda sprawls over three hundred acres of most beautiful hillside and hilltop. Swami Kriyananda, the founder of Ananda and a direct disciple of the world-famous Paramhansa Yogananda, with the generous help of very many associates, had to buy this huge property, not for himself alone, but for the spiritual benefit of a whole community.

"Swami K. shares Gurudev Sivananda's flair for inviting talent and creating a fruitful field for its development. Farmers, printers, carpenters, architects, and artists have all been drawn to him, and he creates opportunities for them to develop to the greatest advantage to themselves and to the Ananda Community. They are given almost total freedom to operate within the Ananda framework, to engage their own assistants on payment of wages, to market their produce and reap and share the profits with the community. They buy, process, and market incense and oils. They make and sell cakes and sweets. One young man manufactures a unique type of jewelry, enshrining beautiful little wildflowers in resin.

"Swami K. calls it the Ananda Co-operative Community, but it is not just another cooperative farm (what would be called a Kibbutz in Israel). It is really and truly an experiment in Divine Life, for everything that happens in Ananda is spiritually oriented. No one is seeking private profit, though profit is not feared. No one is working for material prosperity, though there is no immature anti-materialism. No one goes there to enjoy life, though there is no Maya-phobia. Thus, the silly pastime of ascetics who often fight Maya and materialism which, however, enter by the backdoor, does not occupy life at Ananda.

"Ananda is young (1977); yet already there are over sixty families dwelling there, as also many men and women monastic disciples. The whole place buzzes with activity which, however, is undisturbing and undistracting since the audible silence of the forest absorbs the buzz. Swami K. has worked out to the last detail as it were a delicate balance between freedom and chaos, centralization and disintegration, authority and mobocracy, and has evolved a system of decentralization with the minimum governance from the central authority.

"Swami Kriyananda is young too: he is full of visionary dynamism. The rapidity with which Ananda has grown from almost nothing to its present flourishing state is unqualified tribute to his genius. And, the love and esteem in which he is held by the community, and the total devotion they have for him is beautiful. A young lady member of the community whom the Swami had christened "Shivani" glowed with pride when she showed me around Ananda and repeatedly reminded me, "All this happened in three years." Surely because at Ananda the Divine meets Life! It is Divine Life in living."

Christmas, Easter, and Master's Birthday

Holiday times, especially when Swami was with us, were high points of the year. Easter, Christmas, and Master's birthday were special celebrations, with a particular energy and relevance to our spiritual life. Part of Master's mission to the world, central to the role he played in this lifetime, was to bring back the original teachings of Jesus. At Christmas and Easter, I felt for the first time the deep spiritual inspiration I had hoped all my life to experience at these special times. Finally! I could sense that these were deeply spiritual holidays — true holy days. There was a wonderful vibration at Ananda during the holidays. Though Swami had written some Christmas music, we had few writings specific to Christmas and Easter to inspire us. (In the early 1970s we copied one or two of Master's articles about Jesus from the old SRF magazines. In 1975 *Man's Eternal Quest* was published with several more related articles.) More writings and music were to come in time, especially with the *Christ Lives Oratorio* in 1984. Even before Swami had created music and writings specific to Christmas and Easter, we felt, just as we had in the early years, deep inspiration simply through our life with Swami and through our deepening daily meditations.

EASTER

Easter would begin with a sunrise meditation led by Swami at the Meditation Retreat. Then came a simple breakfast, followed by an Easter egg hunt in what we called Easter Meadow. Hidden in the small meadow were both traditional decorated eggs and spiritual Easter eggs, oval cardboard discs with hand-written inspirational sayings. Swami would give a special Sunday Service talk focusing on Master's teachings on Jesus and what his life represented. The substance of these talks is now available in Swami's 2007 book, *Revelations of Christ*.

CHRISTMAS

Christmas was for me the most inspiring time of year. On December 23rd, we attended the eight-hour Christmas meditation at the Retreat. (When we outgrew the Retreat temple the meditation moved to The Expanding Light.) For a number of years there was a special December 24th breakfast at Swami's dome. Asha led the cooking team; the breakfast was attended mainly by the monks and nuns, as well by Jyotish and Devi and a few others. It was a small, intimate time, with a sweet sense of spiritual family; an intimacy permeated with the dynamic, impersonal vibration of Swami's spiritual presence.

On Christmas Eve, a larger group would gather in the Common Dome at the Retreat. Here we would enjoy snacks, and Swami would usually read us a story by P.G. Wodehouse, one of his favorite humorists. Though we enjoyed the humor and each other's company in a lighter way, Swami's presence filled even such a light-hearted event; the evening was always spiritually powerful and uplifting.

In the Retreat temple, we placed our presents for one another at the feet of the statue of Jesus, his arms raised in blessing. We gathered there again on Christmas morning to celebrate and to distribute the presents. We continued in this way until, our numbers having grown too large, we moved all the Christmas celebrations down to the newly opened, and larger, buildings of The Expanding Light.

My parents came to visit for Christmas in 1975 when the celebrations were still being held at the Meditation Retreat. They had
the full early Ananda experience—outhouses, no electricity and
Swami reading the PG Wodehouse story "Pig Hooey!" Although
they never said much about it to me, I'm sure it was quite a novel
experience for them! At one point in the evening Swami walked
by us and spoke to my parents: "Are you enjoying our Christmas?"
Probably feeling a little overwhelmed by that point, they simply
nodded. The next morning's Christmas Day gift exchange, I feel
sure, seemed more normal to them.

Christmas was very sweet. I did feel the presence of Christ,
mainly through meditation and through Swami's presence. In these
early years, we drew inspiration where we could find it. From the
old SRF magazines Swami shared a few articles about Jesus written
by Master. These articles were doubly precious at a time when there
was so little in print. Our inspiration sprang mainly from meditation, our inner understanding, and Swami's talks on Master's teachings on Christianity and the deeper meanings of Jesus' message.

Here is my diary entry, giving my impressions of Christmas,
1979:

As I sit here on New Year's Eve, I am remembering all the sweetness of Christmas at Ananda. This year was the biggest yet in numbers of people; many of the nuns, myself included, spent most of our
time in the kitchen at the Retreat. The eight-hour meditation this
year was on Saturday (December 22, 1979) and was split between
the temple and the common dome; newer people were in the temple
and the rest of us in the common dome. Swami spent some time in
both places. Josh, a neighbor who is a graphic artist, came and stayed
the whole 8 hours. I was not only impressed, but touched.

On Sunday, December 24, while Swami gave the service, I was
working in the Retreat kitchen preparing for the Indian banquet
on Christmas day. During lunch I sat across from Swami and delighted in hearing about his various plans for people and places. At
one point we were joking about the land deal in which we recently

acquired the Moore's property. Swami said that his offer to Mike, the man who presently owned it, may have been unorthodox, but not unethical. When I started to joke about the distinction, Swami immediately pinned me down and became very serious. He then proceeded to explain to Roger Hodgson (yes, of Super Tramp fame), who was sitting next to me, the difference between the two in this particular situation. He said that he had made no deal with Mike, and therefore didn't feel bound by any previous agreement. Going directly to Mike, the owner, and bypassing Jim, the realtor, was not unethical. Unorthodox, yes, but not unethical. He said that probably most great deals were made in unorthodox ways.

Swami then talked about Europe, and Italy in particular, that we would rotate people from Ananda through Italy, and that Italy would be a steppingstone to India. In this way the vibration of Ananda's presence abroad would be truly international, rather than coming directly from America to India. I have been wondering if I will be one of the ones to go to Europe. We shall see. I feel there is something karmically that draws me to Europe, and yet I can also imagine how difficult it would be.

Sunday afternoon we rehearsed the Christmas choral music—Messiah pieces mainly (Glory to God, Good Tidings to Zion, and the Hallelujah Chorus).

The following morning was the renunciates' breakfast, at which I found out who some of the thirty-nine monks are. Quite a crew! We exchanged gifts, ate, meditated, and listened to Swami singing. Very pleasant despite the fact that there were more than forty people there! Swami gave us his Christmas present—a book of his songs and poems titled Winging on the Wind—very beautifully done and so thoughtful of him. Earlier in the week we had collated the book at the print shop. He also gave me a little jar of jam and a postcard of the Vatican. When I thanked him, he just said so sweetly, "Just a little something extra." He has the great ability to fill even the simplest of things with God's sweetness. After the breakfast we returned to the Retreat for another rehearsal and then Christmas Eve was upon us!

All this time it was pouring down rain, beginning Sunday morning and ending Tuesday night—very messy! The temple and common dome were jammed. It was nice to have Josh and Annie with us again. The chorus, solos and tableaus were very sweet. When I could catch a glimpse of him, Swami looked like he was in heaven, especially when George McClure and Kalyani sang He Shall Feed His Flock. They both have beautiful, sweet voices. We then snacked, Swami read a PG Wodehouse story, we sang a few Christmas carols, and then home.

Christmas Day we (the nuns) left Ayodhya at 6:00 am to cook for the Indian banquet at the Retreat kitchen. I think I was virtually asleep on my feet. We actually had a wonderful time in the kitchen, and I doubt there would have been room for us anywhere else! We cooked right up to the time the meal was served. Then I went into the temple and found my bag of gifts to open. The exchange of presents is always very nice, and yet each year it gets more overwhelming in volume. But it is nice, every so often, to express your friendship for others in this way.

Swamiji is amazing in his stamina! That evening he had people over to his house to see the slides of Romania and have tea and goodies. I went for his darshan mainly and also to see those beautiful slides once again. Suresh was there making tea, so I just started in helping him. Prakash began serving, looking like a waiter with his tray and napkins on his arm. It was a very nice evening.

Just before leaving, I mentioned to Swami that I was going into seclusion and asked for his blessing—which he lovingly gave me.

Since then, I have been secluding and experiencing all the uniqueness of that state. It is never boring, that's for certain! I had been feeling for some time that I was getting out of balance, but I find that only seclusion—meditation, silence, and introspection—really shows in a clear light what specifically is wrong; and also, what the needed corrections are. The funny thing is that those needed corrections are probably glaringly obvious to others, but only with spiritual training do we learn to see clearly within ourselves how we need to change.

MASTER'S BIRTHDAY

Of all the Ananda events, Master's birthday had the most celebratory feel. From 1975 on, at Swami's suggestion, we took our celebration of this event to San Francisco to share with others. We rented a large room and the kitchen in the Unitarian Church at Geary and Franklin, bought the food needed, and prepared a large Indian banquet to serve after Swami's talk on Master's Birthday. One year the event also featured a performance of the Jewel in the Lotus play. People attended this wonderful birthday celebration from all over the Bay Area.

My Spiritual Evolution Continues: A Spiritual Catalyst

In 1974, a swami from India came to visit Ananda at a time when a number of us living in the community were feeling a deep spiritual longing. Tuning into our longing, he magnetized the feeling even more by the way he spoke to us. And he did so during a time when Swami Kriyananda was away traveling. Some of us, I among them, were somewhat caught up in his energy. That fall, when I sought Swami's advice, he responded that he wouldn't feel good about sending anyone to what he considered to be a lesser spiritual path. But he also said it was up to me to understand this for myself. Soon after, Seva asked me if I would like to move to Ayodhya and join the nuns there. When she offered this, I realized that this was what I had been looking for without understanding it—a way to make a deeper spiritual commitment to this path. Through Swami and with the support of my gurubhais, my questioning was answered.

I Move to Ayodhya and Join the Monastery (January 15, 1975)

My decision to make this move may seem spur-of-the-moment, but it had actually been growing inside me for some time. In

December 1973, I had requested a meeting with Swami. At that point, I told him that the only way of life that made sense to me was that of a monastic. Because I was still in a relationship, Swami advised me to continue what I was already doing. He understood my feeling but didn't want me to pull out of an existing commitment. Later, when the relationship was at an end, he thought being at Ayodhya would be good for me. What I wanted most was to focus completely on the spiritual path — to dive into the teachings, meditation, and selfless service. I felt that immersion in the spiritual life was the whole reason I had come to Ananda; living at Ayodhya would provide the perfect opportunity to do so. In January 1975, I bought a bus from a Farm resident, moved it to Ayodhya, and lived in it there for the next seven years.

From my new home in the monastery, I could look back on my two and a half years at Ananda and truthfully say that I had enjoyed all that I had experienced so far. I had gotten settled in the community, I had started Master's Market, and helped build a house, all within the first year of arriving. Now I began my life as a monastic. For the next ten years, I lived very strongly in this monastic consciousness. To me, and to many others at this time, the choice to live as a renunciate came naturally. Swami, himself living in a monastic consciousness, guided us in this way of life, emphasizing what was important and what wasn't. From 1972 to 1980, Ananda's monastery was a strong focal point spiritually. The monks and nuns were generally those people who were most free to serve — to do whatever was needed. And there was a lot that needed to be done for the community simply to survive! Free from family and relationship obligations, the monastics could move about more easily. And move they did! During the beginning and somewhat chaotic years, when the vision of Ananda was only beginning to unfold, the monastery provided one important expression of this vision, especially in keeping the spirit of renunciation alive and clear.

Many of the monastics actively helped build the community on the physical plane, served in the Publications building and print shop, worked at the Meditation Retreat, and accompanied Swami and played support roles in his lecture tours. For those who were involved in these ways, it was a wonderful time spiritually. We could focus completely on the spiritual path, on the teachings and on how to live them in daily life. We also spent a fair amount of time with Swami. Often, he was with us in ways that were simple and sweet—perhaps going out to eat, or to a movie, or to buy camera equipment—times that were also lessons in how to live the spiritual life in every circumstance.

At one point, the monastery at Ayodhya had over 50 monks and nuns. These years, wonderful in themselves, provided also priceless spiritual training for the many who eventually moved on to being married. Those who were involved in the earliest years of the monastery included Binay, Haridas, Jaya, Sadhana Devi, Seva, and Shivani. Among the women renunciates next to come were Anandi, Arati, Asha, Parvati, Vairagi, Uma, Jeannie, Catherine, and Maria McSweeney. Among the men next to come were Nitai, Keshava, Prakash, Prahlad, Vijay, Dinanath, Bharat, Ram, Agni, and Dayanand.

During these early years Swami put a lot of energy into the monastery. Many of us were actively serving the work and, in doing so, were learning from Swami's example the basic attitudes and qualities of the spiritual life. I found that living as a monastic enabled me to live more in the consciousness of being simply a soul, free from self-identifications such as man or woman, young or old. Seldom did I think about myself in these ways. When someone asked me how I felt, I thought, what a strange thing to ask! Who cares how I *feel*. What I really care about is how I can serve. It was a unique time in Ananda's evolution, a time to experience, through attunement with Swami, an impersonal way of life. For me, it was an experience of great spiritual benefit.

Essential though the monastic spirit was to Swami's vision for Ananda, his broader vision was for a true World Brotherhood Colony, as Yogananda had envisioned. To this end Swami worked closely with Jyotish and Devi and with other married couples who were crucial to Ananda's future and to the community's overall development.

Marriages in 1975

In the spring of 1975, two marriages took place: Jyotish and Devi on March 27, and Shivani and Arjuna as well that year. Swami led each of these ceremonies in the Meditation Retreat temple.

Jyotish and Devi's wedding had a distinctively strong vibration of spiritual dharma, duty, and commitment — a consciousness that I hadn't felt at the other Ananda weddings I had attended. I was inspired by what felt to me like the beginning of a new consciousness about marriage.

Based on Paramhansa Yogananda's ceremony, the wedding followed Indian tradition. There was a fire ceremony, the groom leading the bride seven times around the fire. The vows were in Sanskrit, one vow spoken by the groom to the bride with a slightly different vow by the bride to the groom. For the ceremony itself Swami used the words Master used. It was in this way that the early weddings were performed: Jaya and Sadhana Devi, Jyotish and Devi, Arjuna and Shivani, and Hriman and Padma. These weddings, led by Swami, marked the beginning of a spiritual householder way of life at Ananda.

With some couples, Jyotish and Devi among them, the spiritual householder way of life took hold immediately. Together with their son, Kalidasa (born in June 1976 just 11 days before the big fire), Jyotish and Devi lived and served at the Farm. From the beginning, they were a mainstay for the residents there, helping them develop a deepening level of attunement with Master, Swami, and this path.

Arjuna and Shivani lived on the new land just off Tyler Foote Road. As a contractor, Arjuna developed Ananda Construction, which went on to build many of the homes at the Farm. Alone among Ananda residents at this time, because they lived near the road, Arjuna and Shivani had electricity! Arjuna had also managed to hook up a television antenna well enough to get some reception. That year, 1976, we were able to go to their house to watch the Olympics! Most of us hadn't watched television in years (except perhaps the viewing required when visiting relatives!). We did find it fun to gather in front of a TV screen for this one-time event. But beyond that limited exposure, we had no time or interest in this kind of entertainment. There was too much of much greater importance going on in our lives. We were involved in the building of Ananda!

Mohini, Sue Corwin (1975–1978)

I want to write about Mohini because she is one example of how Swami tried to help those who came to him, no matter what their troubles might be. Mohini first visited Ananda during Spiritual Renewal Week, 1975, and asked Swami for spiritual help. Afflicted with a deep-seated mental imbalance, Mohini's inherited wealth undercut her motivation to do anything about her mental condition. What she did have was the good karma to remain at Ananda for several years. During this time Swami and others tried to help her, sometimes going to great lengths to care for her. Perhaps because she had always had a lot of money, she seemed to have little regard for her wealth. On one occasion, Mohini casually withdrew $12,000 in cash from a bank in town. Stuffing the money into a brown paper bag, she walked out onto the streets of Nevada City!

When she wasn't struggling mentally, Mohini was a markedly generous person. During her time at Ananda, we heard someone wanted to buy astrological bangles for all the renunciates who didn't yet have one. Several weeks later fifteen bangles arrived. Though the bangles were given anonymously, we suspected Mohini to be our benefactor. I received my bangle on an early morning in February 1976 on the porch at Master's Market. Swami arrived as I was opening the Market and asked me if I was one of those receiving a bangle; when I said yes, he took one of several he was wearing on his arm that day (to bless them) and gave it to me. I have continued to remember Swami's blessing at this time, as well as to remember Mohini and her generosity to us through the gift of this bangle.

The level of care Mohini needed intensified dramatically in 1977, not surprisingly, during the seven months Swami was away from the community, traveling to Europe and then on India for a four-month seclusion in Kashmir. As he was leaving, Swami asked a number of the nuns to look after her — to try to help her remain at Ananda. I think he felt that being at Ananda would protect her from some of her negative karma. During those months, each morning Mohini walked to work from Ayodhya with the nuns (a one-mile walk!); at night someone usually stayed near her. She was not easy to care for, often figuring out ways to elude those helping her. When in the fall of 1977 her mental health improved, she decided to return to her previous home in New York City. Mohini left Ananda just before Swami returned. When he heard, Swami was saddened but not surprised. Many months later, on June 26, 1978, we received a call from a friend of Mohini's saying that she had ended her life. Swami told us that he had feared this outcome. When we asked him what her suicide meant for her spiritually, Swami said that her action was serious, but that because of her unbalanced state of mind the karma she had drawn from this action would be mitigated. Later that day, on Pubble hill, we had an Astral Ascension ceremony for Mohini. Throughout the rest of the day, I focused on sending her uplifting energy. Though she died in a confused state of mind, I hoped that the help Swami gave her, as well as her own good spiritual karma, would help her — especially as she continued her ongoing spiritual journey in lifetimes to come.

Chapter 3

Ananda Expands! (1976–1978)

 *Thou art the food, and when I break my fast*
Of nightly separation from Thee,
I will taste Thee, and mentally say:
God! God! God!

The expansion of Ananda happened after three major events took place, one after the other. At the time, I don't think I realized what tremendous changes would come from them.

But Swami Kriyananda certainly did.

These events included:

A devastating forest fire in June of 1976 which burned all the homes at Ananda Farm

Swami completing the writing of *The Path*, and its publication, 1976–1977

The Joy Tours, 1978

Looking back on these events, they remind me of what happened to Paramhansa Yogananda in 1941, the year the Golden Lotus Temple at Encinitas fell into the ocean. After that event, he began establishing a number of other Centers in the southern California area: San Diego, Long Beach, and Hollywood Temple to name a few.

Swami Kriyananda acted in a similar way. He knew that the expansion of Ananda would be needed if it was to play an active part in fulfilling Master's mission. But the necessity for this expansion moved more quickly when the 1976 fire happened and threatened Ananda's very survival.

Writing The Path (Spring 1976)

Swami's energy in 1976 was focused on writing *The Path*, the story of his own life, especially of the time he spent with Master. That spring, one evening a week, we would gather in Swami's dome to hear him read to us, by the light of an Aladdin lamp, the most recent chapter he had written. For Swami, the time covered by these weekly satsangs marked his most focused writing. For us, sitting on the floor of his dome during those dark winter evenings, the satsangs were opportunities to hear for the first time the wonderful story he was telling. One evening he stopped reading and asked, "What do you think about what I've written?" When no one said anything, he said, "I want you to give me feedback; I need that." He was demanding of us that we give energy to the writing rather than simply taking it in passively. We needed to give back. Feeling that he needed to get away completely to be able to finish this important book, in late spring of 1976 Swami went to Hawaii, where he had been given the use of a condo, in order to dive even deeper into the writing. At Ananda his energy was continually pulled away in many different directions — among them the Publications business, the Retreat, and the schools. And so it was that Swami, deeply immersed in writing The Path, received word that the "big fire of 1976" had swept through Ananda.

The Fire (June 1976)

On June 26, 1976, a thousand-acre fire burned the entire Ananda residential Farm area as well as several adjacent properties. The Meditation Retreat, six miles away, was not affected. I remember the day it happened quite clearly. Saroj Paliwal, a woman visiting from India and a friend of Swami's, was giving Hindi classes at the small farmhouse on Tyler Foote Road. During the class that day I had to leave to pick up a delivery for Master's Market a mile down the road where Mother Truckers Market is now. While I was picking up the food, someone pointed out to me smoke coming up on the road that went toward North San Juan. In those days, whenever we saw smoke, we took it very seriously. At our desks at Ananda, we each kept a backpack with heavy shoes and clothes in case we had to run off and fight a fire. Seeing smoke so close to Ananda, I quickly loaded the van, drove back to the Farm and asked someone to start ringing the fire bell. This would let everyone know there was a nearby fire.

For us at Ananda, this was the fire of all fires. Beginning at 2:00 pm on a windy, hot, dry day, the fire quickly became an inferno, very large and out of control. Despite our efforts to stop the fire on top of Maidu Ridge, it zipped right past us and, blown by the wind, quickly climbed one-hundred feet into the surrounding pine trees. Raging through the community, within the next ninety minutes, the fire burned down all but one of the homes at the Farm.

When we could see the fire racing past us was out of control, we hurried to salvage what we could and help others to do the same—some to workplaces, others to their homes. A friend and I drove a truck from the ridge to the closest homes to alert people and to pick up what we could of their belongings. First came Vidura and Durga's home, then Lakshmi's, then Jyotish and Devi's dome. The fire was so close to all these homes that it wasn't possible to take much. People had at most five minutes to throw what they could in the back of our truck and then leave. We collected clothing, paintings, valuables, meditation gear, and whatever else people could think to grab. It simply was not possible to defend a home from this fire. Everyone had to leave as quickly as they could. Behind us the flames were rushing up into the pine trees, in some places the flames towering one-hundred feet high. Nothing was going to stop this fire. When we drove down the hill from the homes we had just helped evacuate and encountered a locked metal gate, we simply drove through it! There was not time to try to unlock it. As dramatic as this account may seem, the reality was much more so! We had no idea where this fire was going and where it would stop, what would burn and what wouldn't. As the afternoon wore on, one by one we gathered on the Market lawn.

While people were coming together, I started to evacuate the Market. I backed the Market van up to the porch and started loading. My thought was to be ready to drive away at a moment's notice if needed. In a separate vehicle I drove to Ayodhya to gather from each of the nuns' trailers what I could of valuables as well as sleeping bags—whatever we would need for that coming night.

Seva, Asha, and others went to Swami's dome at Ayodhya to gather irreplaceable items from his time with Master.

As it turned out, the fire burned none of our public or business buildings but did burn all but one of the personal homes at the Farm. Surrounded by brush, with no cleared space to act as a fire break, these dwellings didn't stand a chance. What didn't burn were the Publications Building (now Hansa temple), the house on Maidu ridge, the dairy, the Market and other buildings in the downtown area, the school building on the hill, and the residences at Ayodhya, including Swami's dome. The Meditation Retreat was also spared.

And all this happened while Swami was in Hawaii finishing the writing of *The Path*. We had only two phones at the Farm in 1976, a pay phone by the Market, and a phone in the Publications building. Feeling something was wrong that day, Swami called the pay phone. Luckily, someone heard it ringing, answered it, and told him what had happened.

A few of the local firefighters who were available came to help and were able to contain the fire later that afternoon. Ayodhya didn't burn because the firefighters made their firebreak along Sages Rd. Their decision to do so saved Swami's dome, as well as the land and trailers at Ayodhya.

The only casualty that day was the pilot who was flying the only borate bomber available for our fire. In midflight, the pilot had a heart attack and crashed in the nearby forest. Miraculously, no one else was even injured, all the more remarkable for such a chaotic evacuation—fire everywhere, propane tanks exploding, people trying to save what they could.

During the winter after the fire, the one home that hadn't burned was crushed by an oak tree, its fall caused indirectly by the fire's loosening effect on the surrounding soil. Thus, by the end of 1976, every personal home built at the beginning of Ananda was gone. In one day, within the span of a few hours, the beautiful back-to-the-land country feeling of Ananda was gone; all that was left was ashes and smoke. It was incredible. I remember walking to work that morning through green trees, woods, and beautiful wildflowers. By evening only smoldering ashes remained.

To pull our energies together, see if anyone had been hurt, and begin to see how to move forward, that evening we gathered for a satsang on the Market lawn with Jyotish. It had been a devastating event. In the months following the fire, about one quarter of Ananda residents decided to move on. Those who were strong and spiritually committed enough, stayed. The fire thus served as a natural cleansing time for the community. Those of us who stayed, I think, felt we were with Swami no matter what happened, that we would figure out a way to make the community work, a way to rebuild. And in fact, we did rebuild, little by little, over the coming years, into the thriving community that is here today.

In the meantime, and for many years afterwards, people lived where they could—in the barn, in trailers, in the reception center, at the Meditation Retreat, and at the Farm in a number of what we humorously called "temporary structures." And so, it continued until we could rebuild. For rebuild we did, and in a remarkably short time.

My feeling, and, I think, the feeling of those who stayed was, "Well, the community just burned down. Now what can we do to move forward?" The Red Cross came with clothing; county residents also donated generously. Durga, whose home and everything in it burned to the ground, was named the Queen of the Donations as she sorted through them and tried to direct them to where they were most needed.

After the Fire — Earning Money to Rebuild the Community

After the fire there was a strong feeling to go out and make money to rebuild the community! Because the fire had been started by a faulty spark arrester on a county truck, we could have sued Nevada county for millions of dollars. But Swami Kriyananda said no, to do so would only mean higher taxes for our neighbors: "We don't want to be taking our bad luck out on them." To make our way in this testing time, we had to rely on God's grace.

Swami always operated in terms of the flow of energy. The form of energy needed if we were to rebuild was money. Thinking, as we all were, how to bring in the needed money, in the fall of 1976 I left the Market, leaving Nirmala and Vasudeva in charge, and went with a group from Ananda to work in the rice harvest in Gridley, California. Bharat, who grew up in Yuba City, knew people who worked in one of the rice dryers; buoyed up by his enthusiasm, off we went that fall — our group included Bharat, Kirtani, and myself, along with a number of others.

We shared apartments in a small hotel in Gridley — Kirtani and I happily together in one. Until the rice harvest began, we poled walnuts and did other odd jobs; then, for one solid month we worked seven days a week, twelve hours a day. Because Kirtani worked the night shift and I the day shift at the same dryer, we saw each other only in passing. Our job at the dryer was to test the rice as it came through the shoots. By the end of that month, I knew I was done.

From this adventure we didn't bring home a lot of money, but it was a start!

Another group from Ananda went tree planting in either northern California or southern Oregon. What initially seemed a good idea turned out to mean working in the cold rain and living in soggy tents. The work was demanding but did produce some income.

Service in Publications — Going Deeper
into Our Path (Fall 1976)

When I returned to Ananda later that fall, I was happy to learn that Swami wanted me to set aside any other plans and work in the Publications building. So began the next chapter of the adventure of my life at Ananda.

Work in Publications began quietly with a month typing invoices. Before I describe the dramatic shift that came next for me, let me first say that the central energy at this time was Swami's immersion in the final stages of writing and editing *The Path*. With his work on the book moving quickly to completion, Swami was looking forward to taking a long seclusion in India.

All that year we had been reading chapters of *The Path* as they were being written; I was now reading chapters that I found thrilling. I felt myself getting a much deeper feeling for who Yogananda was. As I read, I felt myself connecting with Master directly. *The Path* carried a palpable feeling of his vibration and consciousness, on a level I hadn't previously experienced. Though I had been on this path for the past four years and was trying to tune into Yogananda through daily meditation and study, it was only in reading Swami's book that I felt, *for the first time*, that I was meeting Master face-to-face and fully appreciating his vibration. It was a thrilling experience.

Swami was in a very deep state during the writing of *The Path*. Remaining inward, he spoke little as these writings continued to pour through him. I had read some of Yogananda's original lessons, some of the original magazine articles, and had heard his voice in, I believe, the only tape recording we had. By meditating deeply on his words and voice, I had felt his vibration. With this experience in mind, when I read what Swami had written, I knew what I was reading was not just Kriyananda speaking. It was Yogananda.

The chapters in *The Path* about Swami's years with Yogananda were a fulfillment of what I had directly experienced from Swami. From the beginning of my time at Ananda, Swami always encouraged us to take the Self Realization Fellowship lessons. Toward the end of my study of these lessons, in January 1974, I even took Kriya initiation from Brother Anandamoy in San Francisco at the Palace Hotel. This experience reaffirmed for me that I had made the right choice in coming to Ananda. SRF's expression of Master just wasn't for me. Swami never wanted to limit us; rather, he wanted us to have our own experience of SRF so that we could compare and choose for ourselves.

It was thrilling for me to feel again, in reading the chapters of *The Path* about Swami's time with Yogananda, the sweetness, the vibrancy, the power, the depth and the subtlety of Yogananda, just as I had felt when I first read the *Autobiography of a Yogi* in 1971.

Swami, speaking of his upcoming travel to India, mentioned wanting to take with him Seva and Vijay Girard. This would be for the whole trip, both Europe and India. How wonderful it will be for them to travel with Swami, I thought. Then came the thought, "If Seva goes, I wonder who will do her job while she is away?" — an important question since she would be away for seven months. As long as I had been at Ananda, Seva had done all the accounting — she was the one holding everything together financially. Her role was crucial; Swami considered her — together with Jyotish — his "right-hand man."

One evening I went to Asha's trailer and asked her what she thought would happen with Seva away for so many months — who would do her job? Asha smiled and said, "Well, we were thinking that you might do it." I was absolutely shocked! I laughed, more in hysteria than amusement. I knew nothing of accounting and had no experience in financial management. I had been at Ananda only four and a half years. But, as it turned out, what Asha had said to me is exactly what happened!

For the seven months Seva was away, I took over much of the accounting work she did each day. I was responsible for the checkbooks (which all lived in my desk drawer) for the various areas of Ananda. Most challenging for me was being the one who had to say "yes" or "no" to those who came asking for money for various Ananda projects.

When I was first faced with this responsibility, I didn't see how Ananda's finances could hold together with Seva away. Lacking any other option, I went into non-stop training with her for the next several months. Swami's original plan to leave in January or February of 1977 threw me into a near panic; such an early departure would allow me only one, or at most two, months training. Fortunately for my state of mind, getting *The Path* ready to send to the printers took longer than anticipated. Swami's departure was pushed forward to April.

To my great relief I was able to spend more than three months working every day with Seva. Our workdays alternated between serious effort and laughter. The laughing is what helped me the most. It loosened me up enough that I could relax into the flow of doing her job in a way that made sense to me and one that my logical mind couldn't imagine. But I also felt, that on a deep level, Seva had somehow given me her brain for the time she was away—the understanding, at least until her return, of how to be an accountant.

In April 1977, the group and Swami departed, everyone together for the European leg of the journey. Then Seva, Vijay, Lakshmi, and Lakshman would go on to India with Swami. When Swami entered into his several months of seclusion in Kashmir, only Seva and Vijay would remain with him.

Publishing *The Path* (1977)

Swami left us to do the actual publishing of *The Path*. He had done his part—the writing; now we were to do our part! Asha was in charge of this very large project—proofreading, typesetting, printing—all in a time when the technology involved was, compared to what exists now, still in the dark ages. The typesetting was doubly difficult because the typist couldn't see what was being typed—the words came out in symbols on a tape. Kathy Mohr, an excellent typist, sat all day long in the Publications building typesetting the six-hundred-page manuscript. Already during Swami's writing, Asha had retyped the manuscript as many as twenty times.

The only place the typesetting tape could be printed out for corrections was in San Francisco; once a week we would take what Kathy had typed to a studio south of Market Street in the city. Staying overnight we would print out the gallies, hang them up to dry, proof them, then drive them back to Kathy at Publications for corrections to be pasted in. Going through the process (of printing the gallies in San Francisco) with Anandi one night brought an invaluable understanding—an appreciation of the energy it takes to publish such a book. It was an amazing time.

Once the book was finally ready for the printers, we held a special ceremony downstairs in the Publications building to bless the manuscript and send it safely on its way.

The Joy Tours

Before his return to Ananda in the Fall of 1977, Swami let us know he wanted to go on two nationwide tours of America in 1978, one in the Spring and one in the Fall. *The Path* was printed, and we had copies in hand. Now, Swami felt, was the time to get it out! Though we had little time to prepare, we understood the urgent need for the tours—not only to get Master's message out but also to draw more people to Ananda to help us rebuild. And so, it all played out.

During Swami's 1978 tours Asha managed Publications and I played a supporting role by managing the print shop, replacing Arati, who would be traveling with the tour group. We printed the literature and posters for the tours and raced to get the materials to each city before Swami arrived. On our Heidelberg press we were able to print beautiful four-color posters with Swami's photograph. All of us involved were caught up in the wonderful energy of the tours.

Swami sent Santosh and Prahlad ahead as an advance team—to book halls and set up media appearances for him.

Vidura drove the motor home which Swami had purchased specially for the tours; Narada drove the rest of the group—including

Durga, Vasudeva, Arati, Maitri, Prita, and Kalyani—in a van they named Chela. The tour group Swami chose were to be representative of Ananda—as well as those who could sing, sell books, and interact with the people who attended the events.

In each city, the whole group stayed with devotee friends of Ananda. Seva, to my relief, had returned from India and would handle the necessary financing for the dozen and more members in the tour group. Funding the tours would definitely require creative financing!

The first tour began in January 1978 in the Bay Area; there Seva and I joined the group for ten days. When they moved on to Southern California, we returned to Ananda to provide support from there. The tour group traveled south to Santa Barbara and Norman Paulsen's Sunburst community, then to Los Angeles. Turning east they drove to Phoenix, Santa Fe, Albuquerque, Houston, and Dallas. East Coast events included Washington DC, New York City, Connecticut (the Satchidananda ashram); then west to Pennsylvania., Chicago, St. Louis, Ohio, Denver, Salt Lake City, Reno, and back to Ananda. In the fall of that same year, the second tour crossed the country in the opposite direction.

Swami's tours promoted not only *The Path* but also the Ananda community. Many were drawn to Ananda after attending a lecture: Krishnadas came from Houston; Latika and Dhira from Washington DC; Dave and Rick Warner, Hassi, and Rich Bazan from Illinois; Maghi and Vasanta from Southern California.

The year before the tours (1977) as well as during the tours, we were beginning to rebuild homes lost in the 1976 fire: several domes in Ranikhet cluster (in 2023, still lived in), including Jyotish and Devi's and a double dome built for a family. Help came from other spiritual groups: Steven Gaskin's The Farm in Tennessee; a Sikh group of carpenters from Yogi Bhajan's group in San Rafael, California; Norman's community in Santa Barbara; and Satchidananda's ashram in San Francisco. We were all touched by the thoughtful and generous spirit of all those who came; their service to Ananda was *very* helpful.

Ananda Sacramento Begins (Fall 1977)

It was also in the fall of 1977 that Swami, again feeling that it was a time for Ananda to reach out more broadly, asked Vijay Girard and Haridas to move to Sacramento and start a center there. He wanted Ananda to begin serving people not only through the Ananda community and retreat in the Sierra foothills but where they lived in the city. The idea was for Haridas and Vijay to rent a house suitable not only for classes and holding Sunday Services, but also for those drawn to ashram living. Though these two Ananda pioneers began knowing no one in Sacramento, they continued until the center/ashram became a reality. Today Ananda Sacramento is our oldest community and is thriving.

Richard Wurmbrand's Talk (January 27, 1979)

The following is my description of Richard Wurmbrand's talk which was a deeply moving experience:

This past weekend, on Saturday evening, January 27, 1979, Richard Wurmbrand came to Grass Valley and spoke at the North Star Christian Academy. Swami Kriyananda and about seventy Ananda members attended. It turned out to be a remarkable evening, a beautiful experience. Swami had met Richard Wurmbrand some years before in Switzerland. Seeing Pastor Wurmbrand as a saintly man, Swami had spoken to us about him several times. (For his faith, he spent at least fourteen years in solitary confinement of the most brutal kind in Romania. With wry humor, he said of himself that he was persecuted first by the Nazis for being a Jew, then by the Communists for being a Christian.)

The speaking area that evening was divided in such a way that, for most of his talk, Pastor Wurmbrand spoke directly to the Ananda group, and mainly to Swami; the rest of the audience was seated behind him. Swami had spoken with him briefly when he first arrived and again before the dinner served by the Academy. Swami said to us, "I told him the name of our community was

Ananda. When I started to explain what the word means, Pastor Wurmbrand, his face becoming dark, responded, 'I know what it means.'"

The following conversation then took place:

Richard Wurmbrand: "Do you believe that Jesus Christ was the Son of God?" Swami: "Yes."

RW: "What do you think of the Muslim faith?"

Swami: "There is good in it."

RW: "But they deny Christ."

Swami: "But there is ignorance in all religions and yet there is good there also. But you are making me defend something that I am really not in agreement with."

RW: "What do you think of Hitler? Was he an evil man?"

Swami: "He was a man who did evil, but he was a man."

At that point Pastor Wurmbrand was called away. When Swami related their exchange to us the following evening, he said that he had thought that, because of their conversation, Pastor Wurmbrand might lambaste us during his talk.

Before the talk, Swami also met Pastor Wurmbrand's wife, Sabina. Speaking with her partly in Romanian, Swami bought a large stack of books. During the dinner, Pastor Wurmbrand came into the room where we were dining just to say hello. Swami was immediately on his feet and walking toward him with a respectful and childlike attitude. Pastor Wurmbrand stayed only briefly, waved to all of us, then said to Swami that they could talk later.

A little later Sabina entered and came over to Swami. She was her usual sweet self. Then, right before Pastor Wurmbrand spoke, Swami, Kalyani, and Lakshman (Simpson) were invited, I assume by Pastor Wurmbrand, to sing "Looking for a Friend."

As Richard Wurmbrand spoke, he focused more and more on Swami (I happened to be sitting directly behind Swami), until I felt that his words were directed almost exclusively to Swami. This evening Richard Wurmbrand was much more joyful and lively than when I had seen him at a previous talk several months before. Whenever he would begin to be preachy or scolding, he would pull

right back. I think, and I believe Swami said this also, that he did
so because he could feel that we all agreed with what he was saying,
that there was no resistance from us.

The entire room felt electrically charged to me with a powerful
joy. All of us, and Swami especially, seemed to draw out of Pastor
Wurmbrand deep veins of thought. He was describing at one point
being in solitary confinement thirty feet below ground—no sun,
sky, birds, or human voices. The guards there wore felt-soled shoes.
There was absolute silence. He said that in that deep silence there
was a sound that was more beautiful, more powerful than anything
he had ever heard. We could feel how moved he was in relating this
experience. Looking directly at Swami, with most of Ananda as his
audience, Pastor Wurmbrand was describing something we were
familiar with through the teachings of yoga, and through our own
meditations. Though Richard Wurmbrand himself did not know
how to more fully understand what he had experienced, what he
did know was that the beautiful sound was from God.

Several times during his talk he urged us to forget ourselves,
to forget this "I," so that "He" (Christ) could come into us and
become our "I." Richard Wurmbrand was deeply moved as he said,
"He acts through us." We were right with him as he described experiences straight out of Vedanta and the teachings of yoga.

He spoke of a man who has been in prison for forty-five years, a
man who could be free tonight if he would just say three words—"I
deny Christ." "But," Richard Wurmbrand went on, "it would be
impossible for that brother to say those words because he has so
much love for Christ. In fact, there is so much love that Christ has
become him—and so who is there to deny whom? Who is there
to deny?" When he reached this point, Richard Wurmbrand was so
moved that he was running his fingers through his hair. And I think
the thrill of describing this great brother in prison was magnified
by sharing it with the large Ananda group who were all so deeply in
tune with his thoughts and his consciousness.

And all the time Pastor Wurmbrand was talking directly to
Swami.

At one point, toward the end of his talk, seeming to tune in to our physical presence in the audience, he mentioned that he understood that we were all from a commune. Then speaking directly to Swami, he said — "But all your women are beautiful! Do you only accept beautiful women?" Swami said, "No. They become so."

Richard Wurmbrand spoke only a little longer. Then everyone headed to the book table and the evening ended.

The next evening, on Sunday, we were with Swami briefly in the motorhome after an afternoon talk he had given in Sacramento. When Seva asked what he thought of Richard Wurmbrand, Swami replied that he liked him very much. The kindness he felt toward Wurmbrand came in part from feeling deeply the great suffering this saintly man had endured.

For those of us who accompanied Swami, the experience of being with Richard Wurmbrand, especially in his interaction with Swami, was thrilling on a deep spiritual level.

Superconscious Living Classes Begin (1979)

Swami, continuing his outreach in 1979, moved into an apartment in San Francisco. In May, perhaps building on ideas that came to him during the 1978 Joy tours, Swami launched Superconscious Living (SCL) in San Francisco's Palace of Fine Arts. The intention was to reach a broad audience by applying the ancient teachings of Raja Yoga to a wide variety of interests — including business, community life, and the arts. Though the turnout was perhaps 250 people in an auditorium that held 1,000, the energy and sheer scope of Swami's presentation of the teachings filled the hall. This evening was a turning point for Ananda, a major expansion in Ananda's outreach. Swami went on to give several more SCL presentations that same year.

A radical departure from Swami's previous approach to the teachings, the Superconscious Living classes were a way to reach those who felt resistance to the purely spiritual aspect. The focus was, rather, on how to work with levels of consciousness and energy in everyday life for one's own highest happiness.

Speakers came from recognizable walks of life — Mike Hebel, a friend of Swami's and high up in the San Francisco police department; Joan Brown, a well-known artist; Jyotish and Devi, from Ananda itself using, non-sectarian, non-spiritual language to present the principles of energy and magnetism, of breath control and centeredness.

Swami followed up the May SCL launch with weekly satsangs at San Francisco's Unitarian Church at Geary and Franklin (the venue for our Master's birthday celebrations the previous several years). The satsangs magnetized Ananda's presence in the city; they served especially as a way to gauge whether there was enough interest for Ananda to begin something more permanent. Each satsang had its own dynamic: sometimes Swami would answer questions; on one occasion, he incorporated a marriage ceremony into the satsang.

Meanwhile, Prahlad and Suresh had rented a house in the Sunset district near Judah Street and 19th Avenue. Swami asked Jyotish and Devi (with their three-year old son Kalidasa) and a number of others to move into this house. Ananda's work in San Francisco was now underway.

The three-bedroom house became home to as many as seventeen people. Swami himself lived for a time in front of the house in his motor home, connected to the house's electricity by a long orange extension cord.

Ananda House in San Francisco

When the end of summer 1979 found us still without a house suitable for an Ananda city ashram, Swami returned home to the Ananda community. It was at that point that things began to move! A member of the satsang group called from San Francisco with news of a house for rent. The "house" turned out to be a forty-five-room mansion in Pacific Heights. When Swami returned to San Francisco and walked into it, he said the house felt like ours — a response strongly reminiscent of Master's when he first saw Mt. Washington. Swami gathered those who had been actively involved with Ananda that summer to ask if they would like to live in the house together and maintain an Ananda center there. When the response was positive, Swami went from person to person around the room asking what they could give to make the ashram/center a reality. Simply to move in the group needed $12,000 — first and last month's rent at $4,500 per month, plus a $3,000 cleaning deposit. By the time Swami reached the end of the circle, the full $12,000 was pledged.

Swami put Jyotish and Devi, together with those who had stepped forward and pledged their support, in charge of developing the house as an Ananda ashram and center. It would be up to this group to make Ananda House work. Formidable as the undertaking was, Jyotish and Devi had the energy and attunement to succeed, and they were able to find enough additional residents to make the project financially feasible.

Ananda now had an ashram house in Pacific Heights, one of the most exclusive, and expensive, areas in the city of San Francisco.

During the next two years, we didn't see much of Jyotish and Devi at the Village; they were much too busy establishing this new work. I, and several others, did drive down several times — including for the 1979 dedication — to visit them, and to see Jacqueline Snitkin (Jamuna) who was living in the Sunset district.

Traveling to San Francisco from Ananda in those days was like going to a different planet. At Ananda Village we lived out in the country, without electricity or running water, had outhouses, dressed funny, had long hair, and weren't particularly interested in being in the city. Swami saw that it was time — for those who were ready and willing to be part of his new direction — to move energy from our rustic beginnings to meet dynamically the challenge of outreach in the modern world. He did so by starting an Ananda ashram house in a Pacific Heights mansion!

This particular house had been used in 1979 as a "decorator showcase" — each room decorated in a unique way, and by a different interior designer. Originally built at the turn of the century, the house had survived the San Francisco earthquake of 1906. It also had one of the best views in the city, overlooking the San Francisco Bay, Golden Gate Bridge, and both Alcatraz and Angel Islands. We were amazed to think that, for the time being, we could call this remarkable house our home.

I Travel with Swami to Australia (1980)

By 1980 I was feeling a little bogged down with accounting (my present area of service) and was open to doing something new.

In May-June of that year, Swami traveled to Australia for a lecture tour. Pieter Meier, Rosanne Bazinet, and I were invited to be a support team on the tour. Pieter especially turned out to be very helpful to Swami with arranging some of the travel plans.

For two and a half weeks we toured the entire eastern coast of Australia—Sydney, Canberra, Melbourne, Brisbane, Cairns, Green Island (on the Great Barrier Reef), and a rain forest near Atherton. The trip gave me a needed break, broadened my horizons, and, most importantly, allowed me to spend quality time with Swami—to experience at close quarters his dynamic energy and will, and to see how he related to people in many different situations. No matter what happened, Swami was always even-minded and cheerful: One example came when we arrived at the auditorium where he had been invited months before to give the main talk at a Wilderness Conference. We found the building locked up and no one around to explain what had happened. Only later did we find out that our supposed host had simply neglected to inform Swami that the conference had been cancelled!

And Swami's reaction to this strange situation? "Without a breath of censure," Swami and the three of us simply turned around and found a nice place to have lunch.

Here are some of my notes from this trip:

May 24, 1980—We arrived three days ago in Sydney. Every day has been quite full. Two days we spent downtown looking at opals, Australia's national stone—Swami, Pieter, and Rozanne, and Anne Sharpen and Gil Sullivan. Gil, an old friend of Swami's, has visited Ananda several times. I have enjoyed him and Anne very much. Australians in general seem more open here in Sydney, a city of three to four million people. They smile at strangers more readily and even say hello. For all the outward friendliness, however, when I went to pick up Swami last night before the talk, I felt in him the lonely side of touring—the longing for seclusion and yet the need and willingness to be out in public. I find it hard even to imagine Swami's profound level of renunciation.

Sydney (May 27, 1980)

Last night Swami showed the slide show and spoke, answering questions, many about the Ananda community. Before the slide show, he spoke very strongly about the coming hard times and how important community living will be. The one hundred people attending were very responsive. It was a varied crowd—young, old, middle class. I find myself a little overwhelmed travelling with Swami in this way, acting as a secretary, and constant companion. I think my feeling is a form of unwillingness. Nor do I find myself attentive and responsive enough to the constant stream of ideas pouring through him. (He is talking about this very thing right now! The nostalgia for the mud.) I think the only solution is to forget myself and move forward in the best way I can. Swami is putting down notes for a book on the qualities of leadership. I'm impressed with the depth of the points he read tonight to Pieter and me. He spoke also of how the slide show was put together in one week. He said he prefers to do projects in this way—short and intense—to work when the flow of energy for a project is there. Not only is the project completed more quickly, but the end result is usually better. On this tour I have to concentrate on forgetting myself and simply doing what needs to be done. My unfamiliarity with caring for Swami on a personal level is making me feel tense. I must realize that I can only do what I can do! I must stop worrying about what I can't or don't do.

Tonight, Swami is giving a mini seminar on Superconscious Living in Sydney. Gil Sullivan, his wife, and Anne Sharpen are here—such nice people. Right now, Swami is teaching the OM technique.

Sydney to Canberra (May 28, 1980)

We are now in the air, flying to Canberra. These small domestic Australian airplanes have an interesting way of dealing with the smoking/non-smoking issue. They simply have one side of the plane for smoking, and the other side for non-smoking! It doesn't really work, but I guess it's what they feel they can do.

This morning as we were packing his suitcase, Swami said that the reason it is so difficult to get out of delusion is not because of its ugliness, but because of its sweetness. There was a piece of music playing on the radio and he said, "For instance, that piece of music, it has a sweetness to it. And it's hard to give that up for a higher reality, a more infinite consciousness."

Canberra (May 30, 1980)

We are now en route to Melbourne, after two very nice days here in Canberra. Swami and I stayed with a sweet couple, Siegfried and Ingrid Weise. Siegfried, a long-time SRF member, has SRF's vibration and reserve about him. Ingrid is very German, bustling, loving, and full of good energy and sincerity. An interesting thing happened while we were there. During our stay, a young couple came to see Swami and asked if he would marry them. He said he was sorry but wouldn't be able to. Then he suggested, in front of Siegfried, that perhaps, since Siegfried is a longtime disciple, he could do the ceremony for them. But, being a good SRF member, he stammered and stuttered and finally said no he couldn't possibly do so. It was a moment of truth for him, and for all of us, to see his reaction. He wasn't able to bring himself to think of this young couple and their spiritual needs, but only of his inability to act as a channel for Master in this situation.

Canberra is the capital of Australia; its population of less than a quarter million gives it a smaller feel than the cities we have already visited. We had fun visiting the Tidbinbilla Wilderness area, about an hour from the city; there we saw koalas, wallabies, kangaroos, emus, and brilliantly colored birds.

Melbourne (May 31, 1980)

Right now, Swami is speaking to an audience of 150 at

Melbourne State College. Last night he spoke at a local church to more than two hundred. The people here are an interested and quite lively group. People I've spoken with seem deeper than those in previous cities. They are already involved in hatha yoga and realize that much more is involved in the spiritual life.

As we leave Melbourne we look back on a wonderful weekend. Yesterday we visited Jangaburra, about one and a half hours from the city. Here a small group of people are trying to start a center, possibly even a community. Although those involved seem sincere, they seem to have no real experience in what they hope to do. Loosely connected with Findhorn, they fashion themselves after that example—relying heavily on "transmissions" to guide them. The method they are relying on may be a bit presumptuous—too much reliance on "transmissions" and not enough on common sense. The physical plane challenges they face—hilly land, heavy with gum trees and brush, rain much of the time we were there—reminded me of early Ananda and all the mud we had to wade through.

Swami mentioned that he felt that Yogananda could be considered the patron saint of communities. Those wishing to live in community needn't necessarily be disciples; rather, they could look to Yogananda and his vision for communities, and could pray to him for guidance.

Brisbane (June 3, 1980)

Swami is in the middle of a three-hour seminar to an audience of more than 150 people.

I am feeling extremely blessed to be on this tour with him and to see him in action. His energy is powerful, tireless, and always sweet. In all situations and at all times he is *giving* to people—darshan, teaching, chatting—and is very sensitive not to hurt or to cut off energy. Though we are in the middle of a hectic schedule and Swami is *very tired*, somehow the energy keeps flowing. I am reminded of the willing crucifixion undergone by St. Francis and other saints. The suffering they subject themselves to they really can't help doing. Theirs is a painful and joyous renunciation of the self for the Self.

My experience of this tour has been on many levels. I have not felt the glowing joy of previous years; what I am learning is on another level. I have not felt physically well during the first part of the tour; I have been battling tension brought on by my unfamiliar role as Swami's secretary and caregiver. Before this trip I would see Swami only occasionally. Now I am with him constantly—packing his suitcase, massaging his head, shoulders and feet, and fixing food for him. The opportunity I have been given I know to be a tremendous blessing, even if a bit overwhelming. I also realize that this experience will only be meaningful if I can "go and do likewise." In fact, the whole vibration of this trip has been one of joy in the midst of stark reality. A wonderful experience to have!

Cairns (Saturday, June 7, 1980)

Swami is giving a lecture/seminar to twenty members of Val Diakos's group. I find it amazing and instructive to see Swami put out the same dynamic energy regardless of the size of the audience! Each talk is the best he can do at that moment, because in every talk he is giving his all to Divine Mother and Master. During the slide show this evening Swami had trouble with his heart; leaving the room, he rested on a counter in the kitchen while I rubbed his feet.

Green Island/Great Barrier Reef (Friday, June 13, 1980)

We returned yesterday late afternoon from three days on Green Island, a coral atoll situated right on the Great Barrier Reef—the only one of its kind. It is a beautiful spot, with crystal clear waters and wonderful coral gardens. The whole time there we did virtually nothing but soak in the soothing tropical vibrations. Pieter and I went snorkeling, exploring the wonderful coral of the reef. Swami seemed to enjoy just being there and somewhat alone.

The Atherton program was light—after the slide show, Pieter, Rozanne, and I answering questions about the community. We enjoyed a beautiful ride up to the tablelands and down again through the tropical scenery of the rain forests. Catching myself getting a bit lax in serving Swami, I have much more appreciation for what Seva, Asha, and Kalyani do in serving him so closely and continuously.

Cairns (Sunday, June 15, 1980)

What next for mankind? Swami is telling his audiences of an imminent collapse world-wide—economic depression, civil war, global war. He is urging his listeners to buy land, either alone or with others, and to grow their own food. A very strong message and one he has repeated throughout Australia. The time is short; the time to act is now.

Ananda House, San Francisco (Thursday, June 19, 1980)

We have now returned from our tour of Australia; the last few days have been a bit of a blur for me. Swami has continued full steam ahead pulling together the money to purchase opals and generating the energy to sell them. I am continually reminded, through Swami's inspiring example, of the true nature of the spiritual path. There is a sweetness as well as a seeming irrationality in what Swami does that can only come from having an intimate relationship with Divine Mother. She is the One who is directing his every move.

I am still having a hard time with my own energy and actions, but I shall just begin again and again until I succeed. It is a strange time for me. I don't have much confidence in myself right now, but that too will pass as I keep moving forward. Jai Guru!

Just before our departure, Swami wrote a letter to the people in Australia:

June 15, 1980

Dear Friends in Australia,

Our visit to your country is rapidly drawing to a close. It has been a joy to see many old friends again, as well as to meet many new ones. You were all so warmly hospitable to us, and lovingly receptive, that we'll be carrying beautiful memories away with us on our return to America. And if any of the meetings were smaller than some of you had hoped, all of them were meaningful to us, as I hope they were also to you. Thank you for everything!

During these weeks I was sometimes asked what I thought of Australia's spiritual future. Well, I'm not a prophet, but I may be able to sense certain trends in consciousness. Australia's future will be, I feel, glowing. But that glow will be found a little bit down the road. For the present she will have to prepare herself, and some of that preparation may involve stumbling through darkness. It will, however, be a darkness for the whole world, not for Australia alone—a darkness brought on by man's own rejection of the light. Australia itself is young enough, and her population small enough, to adjust relatively easily to the changes that already have begun sweeping over the world. The years directly ahead will prove traumatic in many ways—economically, politically, perhaps even geologically—but the purifying process will be less painful for those countries, as well as for those individuals, who cooperate with the new vibrations than for those who cling doggedly to the old.

For that is what is happening. The pressures that are building up on this planet are rooted in a conflict between old and new patterns of thought and behavior. Those people who refuse to let go of the old will find what they cling to being wrenched from them by force. The tides of change that have entered the world at this time are too mighty to be checked. Humanity can only swim with them, or be broken by them—a victim of their own brittleness.

And what are those tides? Basically, what is happening is that we are moving from centuries of almost total matter consciousness into an age of energy. Even with our dwindling planetary reserves of oil, coal, and gas, the trend is toward *more* energy, not less. Our very discovery of those reserves was due to our growing awareness of energy. In the years ahead this awareness will deepen; we'll explore energy as the underlying reality of *all* matter. The more sensitive our awareness becomes, the more refined will be our energy sources. (Even now, efforts are being made to get energy from sunlight, and from temperature changes in the ocean.) Energy is everywhere; it is our inadequate consciousness of it that has kept us bound to material limitations.

The decades ahead will force us to see things more in terms of flow than of structure. People seeking success in any undertaking, for example, will learn to think more in terms of the energy they put out, and of the quality of that energy, than of the specific tools of success.

Politicians will see more clearly that what makes a country is the spirit of its people, not merely its laws and institutions. Religious leaders will realize that selfless love is more important than mere systems of belief. Mankind is being forced by his own growing awareness to look less to the form and more to the spirit of everything they do. The change will be painful only insofar as he resists it.

Now is the time for attuning oneself sensitively to the inflow of spiritual vibrations. It is too late to sit back and merely hope for the best. A spiritual way of life, and above all a life of meditation, will be your best possible protection during the years to come.

I was happy to find on this trip a growth in the general spiritual awareness of Australians. One thing that pleased me particularly was the tendency I found here to take personal responsibility for one's own life. Years ago, a student in one of my yoga classes asked me, "Which is the most important yoga posture to practice?" "That one," I replied, "which has you standing squarely on your own feet!" Australians, I am happy to see, understand this principle. I would be even happier if I found more understanding of the deeper meaning of discipleship, which demands not a spirit of weak submissiveness, but of *openness*, of concentrated receptivity, and a focus on *inner* unfoldment. But if one must err between too much egoic independence and weak-willed submission, I certainly would prefer the former. For until one determines to make truth his own, it will forever elude him.

I was invited to come here as a guest speaker to the second World Wilderness Congress in Cairns. Oddly enough, having come all that distance especially for that, I was given no opportunity to speak! Yet even before the congress I found myself wondering whether there wasn't another reason altogether why I'd been brought here. Certainly, in terms of my own efforts these days to develop Ananda, a visit to a wilderness congress was a bit of a diversion; I came only because I'd promised to. But what I wondered was, did God have some broader purpose for my coming?

Possibly He brought me here to let people know about Ananda Village. Certainly, if some of you feel inspired to create a similar lifestyle for yourselves, this alone would prove a major benefit from our visit. Spiritual focalizing is a growing need of this age. Villages like Ananda will, I think, help greatly in the focalizing process. Even for people who may never want to join a spiritual village like ours, the ideals that Ananda and other communities bring into focus may help to guide them in their personal search.

There was one thing I mentioned in a couple of my lectures that might be worth sharing with all of you who have an interest in forming spiritual communities. I should preface it by explaining that the divine power often works through specific channels for particular purposes. Hence the tradition of patron saints—a patron saint of sailors, of lawyers, etc. One need not be a disciple of a great saint to draw his blessings on an enterprise.

Paramhansa Yogananda might well, in this context, be called the patron saint of cooperative spiritual villages. He was responsible for bringing the "world brotherhood colony" ideal, as he called it, into the world in this age. I heard him say that he had sown this plan "in the ether," for thousands to pick up. Followers of *any* path would find divine strength and guidance in their efforts to form communities, if they would tune in to the special blessing that he sent out into the world to help bring this important movement into being.

I was asked several times during this visit if I would be giving Kriya Yoga initiation. I had to reply that the time was too short. But if I come again in a year or two—that is, if you all invite me—perhaps I can give Kriya then. Or you could get it from a Self-Realization Fellowship representative, if any comes. To receive it from me, I would ask you to take my lessons as well as the SRF lessons, and let me know how you are doing with the techniques I taught on this trip. I didn't teach the techniques everywhere, nor all of them in any one place, again because of the shortage of time. But they are all available on tape recordings that were made of my talks. Altogether, moreover, the recorded talks comprise what might be called—a bit grandiosely, I'm afraid—my "message to Australia." Discipleship to my line of gurus is also a feature of initiation.

Perhaps in future we shall be able to send a group of Ananda members to Australia to found an Ananda branch here.

Meanwhile, God's joy to you, dear friends. Thank you again for your hospitality to all of us. May you prosper in your spiritual life.

In divine friendship,

Swami Kriyananda

Sitting at the dining room table in San Francisco's Ananda House on our return from the Australian tour, Swami looked at me and said, "Maybe Parvati would like to move down to Atherton [near Palo Alto] and help with the center there." Jerry Haslam was already working to establish this center, which would play an important support role to the bookshop we were buying in nearby Menlo Park. I froze at the thought of moving to Atherton. Though I knew such a move was coming, I simply wasn't yet ready to leave Ananda Village. Nonetheless, Swami's asking me turned my thinking in the direction of serving in an Ananda center—as he knew it would.

Meantime, back at Ananda in 1980, I continued working with Seva. She offered me the opportunity to serve in the recently-developing Village accounting office, but I could feel this service wasn't going to be for me.

A Time of Great Change for Swami

By the end of 1980 Swami had come to a unique point in his own life. When, on one occasion, he came into the Village office where I was working, I gave him my usual hug. He seemed simply not there. He said that he felt he had come to the end of a major phase of his life—in a way, to the end of his life. He had created a community, written *The Path*, gone on nationwide and internationals tours. Now, he said, he was feeling that he would either go into seclusion or leave his body altogether. It was a very serious time for all of us. Everything that he had foreseen for himself in this lifetime he had completed. He didn't know what else to do. By the end of 1980, the community, for him, was a fact; the hardcore process of establishing Ananda was finished. It was a time of great and unknown change for him.

In December Swami left Ananda to go on a cruise in the Caribbean. I thought this vacation would be fun for him. But he said he found it completely boring—the people, the food, everything. It simply wasn't his cup of tea.

And then, everything changed.

A Time of Change for Ananda

In January 1981 Swami went off again, travelling alone, this time to Princeville, on the northern side of the island of Kauai. His mood was of not knowing what he was to do with his life. That was all we knew until the day we heard from Shivani (also there on vacation with her husband, Arjuna) that Swami had met a woman that he was very interested in.

Wow! Now that was really something different. Shivani and Arjuna had met her already. Shivani, in her impersonal way, informed us that Swami had met a beautiful, young woman named Kimberly and was bringing her home to the community. And that's exactly what happened, but it wasn't by any means the whole story.

I would like to pause here to ask you, the reader, to also pause and not come to a hasty conclusion about what was happening with Swami and Ananda. Please consider the following: Ananda by 1981 was a dedicated ashram/community full of souls who had come there to find God. We were not people dallying with the spiritual life, but ones who were deeply committed. We were disciples of Paramhansa Yogananda, a great avatar whose world mission we were part of; we were being guided spiritually by Swami Kriyananda, a great direct disciple of this avatar; we had taken Kriya initiation and had dedicated our lives to living Master's teachings in every way possible. It is from this level of consciousness that we now considered the unfolding new phase of Swami Kriyananda's life.

For many of us, Swami's new direction *was* a dramatic shift. Swami was a *swami*! His lifestyle had been impersonal—monastic in the traditional sense. Now, suddenly, his lifestyle was undergoing a radical change. In the eight years I had been at Ananda, and had known and worked with Swami, I had also always found him to be free in his consciousness, free in who he was, free in his expression, always true to the Truth, but not overly concerned about what others thought about his actions—*as long as he felt they were in tune with Master's will for him.*

It was in this spirit that, feeling a deep spiritual attunement with Kimberly, Swami brought her into the Ananda community. He spoke of Kimberly as his soulmate, a term that he had previously made fun of. Swami explained now that Master also had spoken of soulmate as a spiritual concept, but not very openly, concerned that most people would understand it merely as a romantic or physical attraction, not as a profound soul connection.

On one occasion Swami spoke of Kimberly to a group of monastics gathered in his dome. His words felt to me like a bomb dropped in our midst—not necessarily a bad bomb, but an explosion in our present monastic world, mind-expanding and sudden. Swami's relationship with Kimberly signaled that we at Ananda were about to enter into a time of great change, especially for us as monastics, and even as disciples.

Swami began speaking of renunciation in a new way, one that he hadn't expressed before—as an inner state, not limited to its outward and traditional expressions. I could feel that Swami's new approach to renunciation meant a permanent change for Ananda—*not* a bad change, but definitely exhilarating, shaking us out of habitual ways of thinking. Knowing Swami as I did, I felt that the change would be good for all of us, and for Ananda.

Parameshwari, the spiritual name Swami gave to Kimberly, visited the community briefly in the spring of 1981. That same spring, she and Swami traveled to England with Uma (who had been working with Swami on Kauai when he first met Parameshwari).

Starting in the summer of 1981, on their return from Europe, Swami gave weekly satsangs in which he took all of us, the entire community, through every step of his personal unfoldment and growing understanding of this new relationship—about what was prompting it, how he felt, how he was exploring his own feelings about the idea of soul mate, and how she had inspired him.

Swami spoke about himself, about Parameshwari and himself as a couple, about what this kind of relationship meant for the spiritual path, and about how to apply that understanding. Patiently he worked with us to help us come along with him into a deeper understanding of this relationship—of all it implied for the community, for householders, for monastics, and for himself.

What began for me as a somewhat bewildering experience, became thrilling as I tuned into the expansion of consciousness I felt in Swami. Many of us who were able to go with him through this transformational time were also transformed, I think, by diving deeper in attunement,

This was a time for looking beyond every definition of Swami that had formed in my mind: definitions of how he did things and even of who he was. As I went deeper inwardly, I saw that he was still, essentially, the same person—with the same consciousness that I had experienced from the beginning of my time with him and with Ananda. His essence had not changed; only the outward expressions and forms were different. I continued to feel this same, enduring consciousness throughout the tremendous change taking place around me at Ananda. It was, in fact, a profoundly sweet and expansive time.

That summer ended with Parameshwari and Swami at Spiritual Renewal Week. During the evening of the Indian banquet, at the end of the week, Parameshwari shared with us a beautiful flower ceremony she had created. She felt and looked like a lovely queen.

Right after SRW, Parameshwari and Swami went to the coast to share privately their spiritual marriage vows and to exchange aquamarine stones special to both of them.

Later that fall, sadly, the energy changed dramatically.

Parameshwari and Swami went on pilgrimage to Egypt. Swami was the main speaker for a pilgrimage group hosted by another organization. Also on that pilgrimage were Gitanjali (Deborah

Gregorelli) and Gary and Indira McSweeney, who celebrated their marriage vows along the Nile River. It was during this same pilgrimage that Swami wrote the beautiful Egyptian Suite music, about eighteen pieces in all.

For Swami and Parameshwari on a personal level, however, the pilgrimage did not go well. On their return from Egypt, Parameshwari left to attend to personal and family concerns. She did not return to Ananda. I wasn't with Swami during the time of her leaving, and so must leave that story for others to tell. I had, in fact, moved to Ananda House in early November of that year, and was immersed in the adventures of my new life in San Francisco.

Years later, during the lawsuit Self Realization Fellowship brought against Ananda, and the sexual harassment lawsuit that it spawned, Kimberly turned against Swami, even testifying and accusing him of sexual harassment during her time with him. Fortunately, the entire Ananda community had been a witness to the energy between them during the summer of 1981. Some people had even spent personal time with them as a couple; Uma had traveled with them to England. It was sad to see how during the years since her departure from Ananda, Kimberly had become hardened, willing to betray the love, and joy, and spiritual experience she had had both with Swami and with all of us.

Such is the way of maya.

The Monastery in a Time of Change

And what did this dramatic episode in Swami's life mean for those of us who were living in the monastery? Swami's energy and the magnetism generated by his new direction certainly did affect us all. In the early years Swami had encouraged those of us who could, to live at the monastery for some time—as a way to know ourselves more deeply, and to understand what it means to love God. Some who were newer on the path and who had joined the monastery simply as a way of grounding their spiritual lives, did decide to leave at this point and to seek relationships. It was a natural next step.

I myself continued on as a monastic several years longer. I lived in this monastic consciousness for a total of ten years—years I consider to be one of the greatest blessings of my life. It was during this time that I grounded my spiritual life in deepening attunement with Master and Swami. And the friendships that I developed then with my fellow monastics—Seva, Anandi, Arati, Catherine, Maria, Jeannie, Uma—are friendships that I still have more than forty years later.

From 1981 onward, I lived away from the monastery, serving outwardly and dynamically in the Ananda centers. I loved doing so, especially knowing that Swami seemed to think it was good for me. I could feel too that this way of serving was going to bring changes in my own life.

1972, Swami Kriyananda

1973, A tea in Swami's Dome. An afternoon satsang in Swami's dome. These were deeply inspiring times, even though the inspiration may not show on the faces of those pictured. We were very new to these teachings and trying to absorb them. Parvati and Chris are pictured after Swami, second and fourth to the right.

1973, Inside our house at the Farm. A birthday party, Chris and I are inside our "almost completed" house at the Farm (Ananda Village). I am 27-years old. My parents brought cake and presents and took the photo.

1973, House we built, Ananda Farm.

1981, Master's Market

1973, Inside Master's Market, a visitor with Parvati and Sanjaya

1974, Master's Market, Sanjaya sorting produce

1974, My Parents visit Ananda

1974, Christmas, at Meditation Retreat

1976, The Gandharvas, Ananda's singing group

1976, The Nuns and Nitai. On our way to Sunday Service at the Meditation Retreat. Rambhakta stopped our van in the diggings, poked his head in, and took this photo. It captures the spirit of the time. [LEFT TO RIGHT] Asha, Anandi, Seva, Parvati, Nitai

1976, Christmas, Renunciate breakfast with Swami. [LEFT TO RIGHT] Swami, Parvati, Anandi, Bharat, Nitai, Dinanath, Keshava, Binay

1976, Swami reading *The Path*. An evening satsang at Swami's dome. He was writing *The Path*, was full of joy and reading from the manuscript by the light of an Aladdin kerosene lamp. During those evenings we heard, for the first time, what he had written about his life with Master.

1976, Ananda Community after the fire. We are gathered at the Meditation Retreat for Spiritual Renewal Week after the big fire of June 1976. Pictured are many of those who stayed on to help rebuild the community. At this time, Swami was in Hawaii finishing writing *The Path*.

1977, Summer, Ayodhya Monastery, The Nuns

A summer day under the large oak tree at Ayodhya. Pictured are the nuns who worked that summer publishing *The Path*. Asha was in charge of the publishing; Anandi, indexing and proofreading; Arati, design; Kalyani, Vairagi and Maitri proofreading. Parvati helped with proofreading, but had stepped in for Seva as an overall bookkeeper for Ananda while Seva traveled with Swami to Europe and India. The nuns pictured here worked together at the Publications building and lived in trailers at the Ayodhya monastery. It was a wonderful and deeply spiritual time. [CENTER FRONT] Mohini (in striped shirt), the woman we were caring for that summer. [FRONT ROW, LEFT TO RIGHT] Vairagi, Mohini, Anandi; [BACK ROW, LEFT TO RIGHT] Kalyani, Maitri, Arati, Asha, Parvati

1977, Blessing *The Path*. Downstairs in the Publications building, we are blessing the package that contains *The Path* manuscript before sending it off to be published.

1977, Swamiji in Rome, on the phone to Ananda, speaking with Parvati!

1977, Nuns Retreat Day, Swami's dome at the Meditation Retreat. That summer while Swami and Seva were away, we held several retreat days for the nuns. [BACK ROW, FROM LEFT] Vairagi, Shankari, Arati, Asha, Kalyani; [FRONT ROW, FROM LEFT] Anandi, Parvati, Uma

1978, Monks and Nuns in Swami's dome

1977, November, Swami has just arrived at the Sacramento Airport and is holding a copy of the newly printed book, *The Path*.

1978, Publications Crew. Pictured are a number of the Ananda residents who worked at the Publications Building in 1977. Earlier that year *The Path* had been published, and now were printing much of the material needed for Swami's U.S. Joy Tours in 1978. [FRONT ROW, LEFT TO RIGHT] Kasandra, Arati, Parvati, Prem, Anandi, Tricia, Julia; [STANDING, LEFT TO RIGHT] Rammurti, Jack (our hired printer), Nalini, Snowman!, Durgadas, Jyotish, Mark D., Madhava, Sita, Shoki, Nishtan.

[LEFT] 1977, Publications Building, Downstairs office (now Hansa Mandir). A gathering of some of the women who worked in the Publications building in 1977. [STANDING] Durga; [SEATED, CLOCKWISE] Parvati, Vairagi, Nancy, Tricia, Anandi (her back is to us)

[RIGHT] 1978, Joy Tour, Sunburst Community. Bernard, Norman, Swami

1978, San Francisco, Swami Satchidananda and Swami Kriyananda

1978, Retreat Kitchen dome

1978, Retreat Kitchen. The cooking team working with Asha on a meal, one of many we prepared over the years for special occasions. Always fun to work together, we cooked in the Meditation Retreat Kitchen dome – propane refrigerators, no electricity, all chopping done by hand. [LEFT TO RIGHT] Prita, Uma, Parvati

1978, Inside Swami's Dome
at Ayodhya

[ABOVE] 1978, Inside Swami's Dome

[BELOW] 1979, A *Satsang* in Swami's dome. One of many gatherings in Swami's dome. Pictured are a number of those who were serving Ananda.

1978, The nuns with Swami [FRONT] Anandi, Parvati, Arati, Vairagi; [SECOND ROW] Kalyani, Shradha Ma, Swami, Asha; [BACK ROW] Shankari, Maria, Uma, Seva

1979, May Day at Ananda. A May Day celebration in the open field, now the location of The Expanding Light. Parvati and Arati are in a three-legged race as part of the fun. [LEFT TO RIGHT] Arati, Parvati and Brindey

1979, Christmas with Swami, Meditation Retreat Common dome. Swami is reading something fun to us at an informal gathering on Christmas Eve.

1978, Parvati at Lake Shrine (photo taken by Swami).

1979, Swami in San Francisco. We are visiting Will Knofke with a group from Ananda.

[ABOVE] 1980, A skit looking into the future, May 5, 2002! Meditation Retreat Temple. [LEFT TO RIGHT] Parvati, Arati, Krishnadas, Prita, Seva, Anandi, Devi, Jyotish, Santoshi, Asha

[LEFT] 1980, Australia. In May on tour with Swami Kriyananda. A seminar in Melbourne to about 150 people.

[BELOW] 1980, Australia, Travel group: Rosanne, Pieter, Parvati

[ABOVE] 1980, Australia. Outdoor class with Swami

[LEFT] 1980, Australia, Parvati

1981, On Vacation with Seva. Mt. Washington tennis court

1981, On Vacation with Seva. Encinitas bluff at the Hermitage

1981, On Vacation with Seva. Carmel on the beach, Lakshmi, Parvati, Seva

Chapter 4

Centers and Communities (1981–2004)

 *No matter where I go, the spotlight of my mind,*
Will ever keep turning on Thee.
And in the battle din of activity, my silent
war-cry will be:
God! God! God!

Service Away from Ananda Village

From 1981 to the beginning of 2004, a period of more than twenty-two years, I had the blessing of spending much of my time helping to direct, and even to start, Ananda centers and communities. This wonderful time in my life expanded my horizons, and gave me a direct experience of Swami Kriyananda's vision of Ananda's work, as well as first-hand experience of how he worked with people (myself included).

Ananda communities began where they did in response to the people involved. Because Ananda's focus has always been on supporting individuals in their spiritual growth, it was the desire of individuals for Master's path and teachings that drew us to where they lived.

For me, serving outside Ananda Village was important spiritually. The memory of the experience I gained during these years has remained with me. For it was during this time, especially when I was first in San Francisco, representing Swami, Master, and this path, that I experienced the power of their presence within me most dynamically. I could not have done all that I did in the years that followed had I not felt their energy, power and consciousness flowing through me. So thrilling was this experience that I encourage others who have the opportunity to do so, to serve in this way, that they too may share this blessing.

Ananda House in San Francisco (1981–1983)

1981 was not an easy time for me. Starting in the fall of 1980 I had worked with Ananda Village finances—work that I knew needed to be done, but that was not personally fulfilling. In the summer of 1981, I was asked to serve again with Ananda's print shop, recently moved to Grass Valley and struggling financially. Though others hoped I might be able to help, I found myself unable to resonate with the work and left after only a few months. Without much enthusiasm I returned to doing Village finances, a work that I could feel was coming to an end. Others somehow felt the same and, to my joy, a major and wonderful change came into my life.

In September of 1981, Swami Kriyananda was in San Francisco visiting Jyotish and Devi at Ananda House, where they had been living since the fall of 1979. This house, located in Pacific Heights, just off the corner of Broadway and Fillmore, at 2320 Broadway, was a *mansion*: four and a half stories high, with forty-five rooms and nine bathrooms. Swami's comment when he first walked into it was, "This feels like ours." Jyotish and Devi had spent the last two years developing the house as an ashram for the residents, as well as establishing an Ananda Center in the city. By the fall of 1981 they were feeling the need to return to Ananda Village.

It was at this time that I received a phone call from Purushottama, then visiting Swami at Ananda House in San Francisco. His message: Swami was wondering if I would like to move to San Francisco to help run the center there. Wow! I was shocked, but, at the same time, thrilled and amazed! People often ask how decisions are made at Ananda, especially about who goes where. My own experience is that whenever Swami asked me to do something, the vibration was always one of respect, joy, and invitation—never of command. I always knew I was free to say no if a request didn't feel right to me.

I also felt that, through these requests, Swami was inviting me to be part of the adventure he was living in creating Ananda. I knew it was my great blessing to play a part in this work.

In this particular instance, Swami's comment was that he thought this move might be a nice thing for me. My own feeling was the same. Taking a deep breath, and hoping I was ready (and underneath it all knowing that I was), I said, "Of course, I'll do it." I could feel that it was important for me to move on, to expand my horizons—as I had seen Swami himself doing the same year.

By early November 1981 I had packed up everything I owned (which wasn't much, since I had been living in a bus for the past seven years!) and moved to what was now called Ananda House. The change for me was greater than one might think: I was moving from a bus in the woods, with no electricity or running water, to a forty-five-room mansion located in an exclusive area of San Francisco! In addition, I was now going to be in charge of directing it. For the past seven years I had been living a sweet and simple life with close sister disciples in the woods at the Ananda monastery, just up the hill from Swami's dome at Ayodhya. Further, in all my nine years at Ananda, I had taught only a few classes and given even fewer Sunday services. Acting as a minister and helping others with their spiritual lives were also new to me. Great as the change was, I knew it would be a great spiritual adventure, and I felt ready for it. Somehow, I knew I would love it.

The move to San Francisco was the start of a wonderful time for me spiritually. Although sometimes I felt as though I had been shot out of a cannon, on a deeper level I was ready to test my wings. I felt a great thrill at being sent out—of being asked to go, of saying yes to doing so, of being able to be a dynamic part of this spiritual work. It was not in any way a hardship for me. Significantly, it was only when Swami asked me that I became aware of my readiness. Though he knew the work would be good for me spiritually, it was essential that I also say "yes." If I had said no, then this great spiritual opportunity would have simply passed me by. And I think that my spiritual growth from that point on would have been slowed.

I was thirty-five years old, and astrologically in a wonderfully expansive Jupiter cycle — a time for spiritual adventure. Inwardly I could feel that my life at Ananda the previous nine years had been a preparation for this time. If I was ready, and if I was willing, a great spiritual adventure would unfold for me.

In November 1981 I arrived at Ananda House and began living in the city. I shared a room for the first several months with Michele, one of the original residents of the house. Since space was at a premium, the larger rooms were usually shared. It was an ongoing challenge to figure out who could live with whom.

One of my first outings with Jyotish and Devi was to see the just-released movie, Chariots of Fire. Subsequently, whenever we would go to the Marina for a run along the Bay, I would remember the film's opening scene. I felt that I too was preparing for my own version of the Olympics — to live the spiritual life in the middle of San Francisco.

A Mansion on Broadway

The mansion we lived in had been built at the turn of the century and had survived the 1906 San Francisco earthquake. The large rooms were arranged in suites by the original wealthy family that had built it. The house had been through a number of incarnations over the years, even one as a boarding house. Most recently, just before Ananda's lease, the mansion had served as a Decorator Showcase for the annual San Francisco event: A number of the rooms in the house were done over, each by a different interior decorator, as a way to demonstrate their skills. The results were interesting, greatly varied, and sometimes hilarious — a source of much enjoyment for those who now lived there.

And so began my adventure of living at Ananda House — giving Sunday Service every other week, teaching classes (including a Yoga Teacher Training Course), counseling, managing a forty-five-room mansion with twenty-five to thirty residents, and keeping the house and the Ananda Center at 23rd and Judah Street. financially viable. Fortunately, I wasn't serving there alone!

To provide a transition time of training for me and the other two ministers Swami had asked to join me, Jyotish and Devi stayed on from November 1981 through late January 1982. Ram and Dianna Smith, who were living in the Ananda Atherton Center, were unable to make the move to San Francisco until the beginning of January, and so had a much shorter time with Jyotish and Devi. Swami had also asked Yogindra and Santoshi to move to San Francisco. Their Grass Valley computer business recently dissolved, Swami saw service in this new ashram as a possible next step for them. It was a thoughtful gesture.

Jyotish and Devi Set the Tone

For more than two years Jyotish and Devi had done a wonderful job creating a spiritual vibration among the residents at Ananda House. The overall feeling was one of spiritual family, meditating together and exploring how to live the spiritual life. The residents included single people, and couples with and without children.

The daily routine of the house, established by Jyotish and Devi, served the residents well. Mornings Monday through Friday included a group meditation in a room set aside for the temple. Because people had to leave at different times for jobs or school, breakfast in the dining room upstairs (overlooking the San Francisco Bay) was, except on special occasions, a "make-your-own" meal. Since most people were away from the house during the day, a lunch was not usually served. Each evening at 6:30 a dinner, prepared by a rotating schedule of house residents, was served buffet style in the dining room. For each of the residents there was a schedule of duties that included cooking, cleaning, food buying, and whatever else was needed to keep the house in order and running well.

In the early 1980s we also had a "house" phone bill, a unique experience of group living at that time. Since there were no cell phones, and only one phone number for the entire house, one brave soul had to take on deciphering and billing each resident for the phone calls they had made that month — a true tapasya! It wasn't always clear who of twenty-five residents had made each call, or for what reason.

Spiritual Holidays at Ananda House

Thanksgiving Day came two weeks after I moved in — my first "holiday" event at Ananda House. That morning, we meditated together, then lightly swept and cleaned the house to prepare for the many guests who would attend the meal later that day. As we worked, a lovely feeling permeated the house. Together we made the main dishes, knowing that those coming from outside would bring additional dishes. Once everything was in readiness, Devi said, "Let's make the food look nice, so that when it is served there's a feeling of upliftment." And there was.

Christmas brought a familiar and sweet feeling of spiritual family, similar to what I had experienced with Swami at Ananda Village. This feeling was especially touching in such a diverse group of people, many of whom were still quite new to the spiritual path, and very new to actually living in the spiritual vibration of Ananda House. Jyotish and Devi had worked with the residents to make the life there real to each one. It was wonderful to come into this newly created ashram house.

Serving as a Minister in the City

Before I moved to Ananda House, I had volunteered early in 1981 to do a couple of Sunday services at the Ananda Centers in Sacramento and Stockton. I had felt a need to move in this direction and thought I should test the waters. Officially I became a minister on April 22, 1981, at the Yoga Fellowship meeting. When Swami was told that I was now giving some Sunday services and that perhaps I should be made a minister, his response was simply, "Fine." It was sometimes in this low-key way that members were moved into the ministry. One of the keys to being made a minister was a willingness to take on responsibility, even when not directly asked. Another key was that the new role seemed to others, and especially to Swami, spiritually helpful for that person.

Serving in San Francisco was quite different from giving an occasional Sunday service in a city center. To prepare myself, I wanted to draw on Jyotish and Devi, who had been serving full-time as ministers for years, as much as possible in their remaining time in San Francisco. I went into training mode, attending all Sunday Services, classes, events, everything, knowing that I would soon be one of the people doing it all!

Celebrating Master's Birthday

The first major event Jyotish and Devi asked me to help organize was the celebration of Master's Birthday on January 5, 1982. This event, a major annual event for Ananda, was especially so this year because Swami and many Village residents would be coming, in addition to the residents of Ananda House, San Francisco and those involved in the new Ananda Center at 23rd and Judah. Additional devotees would come through East-West Bookshop (purchased by Ananda in 1980), from the Ananda Center in Atherton, and from Ocean Song near Santa Rosa. Ananda had a strong presence in the Bay area at this time.

As early as the mid-1970s, Ananda began celebrating Master's Birthday in San Francisco each year at the Unitarian Church at Franklin and Geary. Driving down from the Village the night before, we would spend the day of the event cooking a complete Indian meal in the church's kitchen. During the meal Swami would speak to us about Master's life and Ananda's role in serving his work. We invited people from all over the Bay Area to join us for this event. Whether we were there as a guest or as a meal server, our hearts were touched by this wonderful celebration.

Planning for such a large event in 1982, we knew we would need a hall much larger than the Unitarian Church. I thought of the Scottish Rite Hall, where we had heard Swami Satchidananda speak. Not remembering the exact location, I went to a Scottish Rite Hall listed in the phone book as located at Van Ness and Geary. The hall turned out not to be the one I had been thinking of, but still seemed a good choice—centrally located, with street parking available in the neighborhood, and situated at the base of a large building, making it quiet and protected from the street noise outside. I decided to rent it.

It was only some years later that we discovered in an old SRF magazine a photo of Master, with a large audience around him, standing in this same Scottish Rite Hall! His talk there would have been a stop on one of his nationwide tours in the 1920s. Though our renting the same hall Master had spoken in seemed purely coincidental, we couldn't help wondering whether some deeper guidance had been at work!

For a number of years after the 1982 Master's Birthday event, we used the same hall for our annual World Brotherhood Day celebrations. Following the program with Swami, we would accompany him for a special dinner at the exclusive Gaylord Indian restaurant in Ghirardelli Square—a wonderful ending to this blessed evening.

The 1982 Master's Birthday event marked a culmination of the years since 1979, years of spreading Ananda's presence in the Bay Area, and of increasing public awareness of Swami Kriyananda and Ananda. It also marked Jyotish and Devi's last major event before their return to the Village. For me personally this time with them, in training for my new role and simply in spiritual friendship, had been a great blessing.

Swami visited Ananda House regularly during the 1980s, staying in the room kept for his use on the top floor. Because he was travelling frequently, especially to Europe, Ananda House was his regular stop on the way to and from the nearby San Francisco airport. It also served as a home base for many other Ananda events in the Bay area.

The Lighter Side of City Ashram Living

Though our life at Ananda House was certainly challenging, we also made it fun and inspiring. Events held there included specially themed dinners (Japanese, Indian and others), Halloween, Christmas, and films we watched together. Our location was one of the best for viewing the San Francisco Bay, the Golden Gate bridge, and Alcatraz and Angel islands — prime viewing for the annual 4th of July fireworks in the Marina. One evening we had a ballet performance by two congregation members who were with the San Francisco Ballet Company. To prevent the dancers slipping, we covered the entire dining room floor with a mixture of sugar and water. Removing the sticky mixture the next day was an interesting challenge! A classical Indian dancer attended Ananda events, performed at the house, and even taught classes for our residents.

Also memorable were learning to park on the Fillmore hill (one of the steepest in the city!), and Sunday services followed by fresh bagels and cream cheese. The services were held at the Ananda Center in the Richmond district at 23rd and Judah Street. Because the public bus stopped directly in front of the Center, we never knew who might walk in during one of our services.

The Vedanta Society Center was located on Vallejo Street, directly below Ananda House. It was sweet in the early morning to sometimes see one of the orange-robed swamis making his way on foot to the Center along the city streets.

One of the house residents was a local Bay swimmer who had done the Alcatraz to Aquatic Park swim a number of times. She convinced me that I should at least go for an early morning swim with her at the Park. Here a number of brave souls from the local swim club swam each morning. I did join her several times. The water was absolutely freezing but invigorating. On one of the swims, when I looked back from some distance out, the view of the city high-rises in the early morning sun was uniquely beautiful. Relying on a resident who knew how to sail (at least a little), we rented a sailboat in Sausalito and went out on the Bay, then landed on Angel Island for a picnic and hike around the island.

An Ananda Yoga Teacher Training Course
in San Francisco

Before Jyotish and Devi left San Francisco, Jyotish several times suggested, "It would probably be good to start a Yoga Teacher Training Course here in San Francisco." The first few times, Ram and I looked at each other and smiled. Because we had just begun teaching the basic classes, an advanced course was overwhelming to think of doing so soon. We only began to take Jyotish's suggestion seriously when he said to us, "If you don't do this course, you probably won't have enough money to pay the rent on the Center." It turned out that he and Devi had been paying part of the rent out of their own income. When they left San Francisco that income would go with them. We finally understood that the Center had to become *much* more active and income-producing to stay in existence. Starting a Yoga Teacher Training Course wasn't only a good idea; it was essential to keeping the Center afloat.

Since we now understood why this YTTC needed to happen, we simply had to step up to this additional challenge, and quickly! Ram and I learned what we could from Prakash — how he had presented the YTTC in our Atherton and Stockton Centers. Our first Yoga Teacher Training Course in the Ananda San Francisco Center was launched in the spring of 1982, and was a great success. In the early 1980s the idea of yoga training courses was still new; in fact, we may have been one of only a few yoga centers in San Francisco offering such a course. We continued to offer the YTTC three or four times a year from that time on. Early students included Lisa Powers, who drove all the way from San Jose to attend, Gary McSweeney, and Edna Jacobson.

The Ananda Center at 23rd and Judah now offered a wide variety of classes, including our newly launched Yoga Teacher Training Course, as well as weekly Sunday Services. We were responsible for running both the Center and Ananda House. The house needed twenty-five to thirty paying residents to meet expenses. The residents needed a focus and support for their spiritual lives — daily sadhana, fun activities, and classes. Ram and Dianna and I alternated doing Sunday Service; Ram and I focused on YTTC; all three of us gave the classes and provided spiritual counseling for the residents and congregation members. It was a busy time, challenging, and blessed. The blessing of serving in this way we each understood deeply, and with gratitude.

Sunday afternoons were a special time for me. After Sunday service, I usually walked by myself down to the Marina. This was my time, set aside each week, to be with Divine Mother, Master, and Swami — it was a time that I always looked forward to.

Ram and Dianna Smith

I studied hard in the first months of 1982 — especially for the YTTC, the classes, and Sunday Services. More time went simply into being with people and helping them with their spiritual lives. Further time went into dealing with finances, making sure we could meet our expenses each month. It was an intense and wonderful time. Ram's positive energy was invaluable. Eternally confident even when he didn't know what our next step should be, he never worried. Our life in San Francisco was a great adventure — one in which we needed to rely on Master, Swami, and Divine Mother for their guidance and their grace.

Dianna, who was still somewhat new to Ananda at this time, had a wonderful spirit. Newly married to Ram, she was now a co-director with Ram and me. When they first arrived at the beginning of the year, both she and Ram worked part-time outside the Center, Ram doing gardening and Dianna doing office work. After a few months, we figured out how the house and center could financially support the three of us. All three of us were needed full-time! We could now focus fully on classes, promotions, supporting residents and congregation members, whatever challenges each new day brought. We worked well together and greatly enjoyed keeping everything going.

Divine Mother Guiding Our Lives

Yogananda, in the early years of being in America, was once asked, "What are the assets of this organization?" "None!" he replied, "Only God!"

One constant challenge was to keep Ananda House financially viable and its more than two dozen residents spiritually in tune. Because most residents were new to the spiritual path and had not lived in an ashram setting before, morning meditations and the Sunday services were important times for us to come together. To keep our finances viable, we were always on the lookout for additional residents who were on our spiritual path. One day the three of us were meeting and trying to figure out, yet again, how to get that one more much needed resident into the house. As we prayed to Divine Mother to send us the person we needed, the doorbell rang. When I opened the front door, there stood a small, well-dressed, nice-looking woman. She said she was from Brazil, was on this path and had somehow heard about Ananda, Swami, and Ananda House. She would be staying in San Francisco for a number of months. Did we have any rooms available? Yes! We definitely did. She moved in that very day. Another among so many miracles from Divine Mother!

For me personally, the years in San Francisco were a time of great spiritual adventure and growth. And I knew I was blessed to share this time with Ram and Dianna.

It was during the summer of 1982 that two deeply spiritual events occurred.

Higher Kriya Initiations at Ananda Village (July 1982)

The Higher Kriya Initiations were held in July 1982 at the Village—the first time Swami Kriyananda had felt inspired to offer them at Ananda. The initiation into all three higher kriyas came as the culmination of a weekend program focused on preparation. Swami led the ceremony early Sunday morning, then went on to also lead the Sunday Service that same morning. Attending the initiation were about 150 people, mainly from the Village and the Ananda Centers. It was a very powerful spiritual time, with a great deal to absorb from the initiations. Because of this, after the Sunday Service I asked Ram and Dianna if they would be willing to cover my classes in San Francisco for the coming week. I felt I would lose a lot that had been given during the initiations by returning to the city so soon. I did feel somewhat selfish asking this of them, but they graciously agreed.

Ananda Moyi Ma's Transition (August 1982)

A second event that summer was the passing of Ananda Moyi Ma in India in early August. Swami had been very close to Ma, and when I arrived at the Village that summer at the beginning of SRW, he invited a few of us to his dome to meditate with him at this auspicious time. I felt Swami wanted to honor Ananda Moyi Ma at the time of her transition from her earthly body. It had been a powerful incarnation for her; all her life she served thousands of people throughout India, and always upheld the teachings of *Sanaatan Dharma*, the Eternal Religion. Ananda Moyi Ma had, throughout her life, been a living example of this deep understanding of religion that India is so well known for throughout the world.

Here is what Ma replied to Paramhansa Yogananda when he asked her on their first meeting in India in the mid-1930's, "Please tell me something of your life."

> "Father, there is little to tell. My consciousness has never associated itself with this temporary body. Before I came on this earth, Father, 'I was the same.' As a little girl, 'I was the same.' I grew into womanhood, but still 'I was the

same.' When the family in which I had been born made arrangements to have this body married, 'I was the same.' And when, passion-drunk, my husband came to me and murmured endearing words, lightly touching my body, he received a violent shock, as if struck by lightning, for even then 'I was the same.'... And, Father, in front of you now, 'I am the same.' Ever afterward, though the dance of creation change around me in the hall of eternity, 'I shall be the same.'"‡

Here is what Ananda Moyi Ma said to Swami Kriyananda:

"Many thousands have come to this body. None have attracted me as you have."

"There are people who have been with me for twenty-five years and more, but they haven't taken from me what you have."

And what Ma said to others about Kriyananda:

"Here is a lotus in a pond. Many frogs sit under the lotus, croaking. Then a bee flies in, takes the honey, and flies away. Kriyananda is that bee."§

The Adventures Continue

May 1983 and moving forward was, for me, a time of travel, inner growth, and "hacking away inwardly" at what I needed to let go of (a letting go which was, I felt, little by little actually happening).

‡ *Autobiography of a Yogi*, Copyright 1946.
§ From *Visits to Saints of India*, Part 1, Copyright 2007

Serving as Swami's Secretary
(June–November 1983)

By the Spring of 1983, I felt ready to return to Ananda Village. I had been in San Francisco for a year and a half. Still committed to being a nun, I had found it challenging to be in the middle of a city such as San Francisco and mixing with so many different kinds of people. Much as I loved the adventure of it all, living in a city center as a monastic was not easy. I returned to the Village in May; Ram and Dianna continued on as center leaders in San Francisco.

Arriving at Ananda Village in May 1983, not knowing what my next step would be, I moved into a trailer at Ayodhya. The Ayodhya cluster, including Seva's and Vairagi's houses, was just beginning to be built. When I arrived, Keshava, who had been Swami's secretary for the previous five years, was feeling the need for a break; I was asked to fill in for him. From June through November 1983, I functioned as Swami's secretary. Poor Swami! I wasn't very good at the job, but he did survive these five months. For me, needless to say, the time with Swami brought deep spiritual blessings. I was especially struck by the spiritual sincerity of those who wrote to Swami—a memory that has remained with me ever since.

Swami's Mother Visits

It was also during this time, June 1983, that the marriage of three couples took place at The Expanding Light temple: Uma and Bill (Krishnadas), Anandi and Bharat, and Sheila (Naidhruva) and Dinanath. Invited by Uma, who had a sweet connection with her, Swami's mother attended this wedding.

Hosting Swami's mother at the wedding and at other times during her visit, I found Mrs. Walters a beautiful and refined woman. Recently widowed by the death of her husband of fifty-eight years, she seemed somewhat removed from the wedding and all that was happening around her at Ananda. Swami's father had died in February that year (interestingly, on the night of Shiva Ratri);

and Mrs. Walters herself passed away in July 1983 at the home in Menlo Park, California she had shared with her husband. In the last two years of their lives, at Swami's request, Vairagi Escobar lived with them and looked after them, continuing this service right up to the time of Mrs. Walter's passing.

The Building of Crystal Hermitage (Summer/Fall 1983)

With the death of his parents Swami, and his surviving brother Dick, each received an inheritance. Swami's portion was valued at about $250,000, a lot of money in 1983. And what, you may ask, did he do with such a large sum? He quickly began making plans to build much of what you see today as Crystal Hermitage.

Planning began the summer of 1983. Because I was Swami's secretary, I was present at several meetings with some of the architects involved. In the fall of 1983, construction began on the dining room/library and the kitchen wing. I could see Prahlad, Vidura and others working on the foundation in the cold rain. All of the money Swami received from his inheritance went to building what he said would be the "spiritual heart of Ananda." It would be a refined, uplifting, and beautiful place for community gatherings and for visitors. Swami filled the new Hermitage with Kashmiri furniture, Balinese and Indian artwork, paintings from Capri, Italy—works of art gathered during his travels all over the world.

Ananda's Italian Adventure Begins (Spring 1983)

The spring of 1983 also marked the beginning of Ananda's Italian adventure. I was still living in Ananda House when, in response to Swami's invitation, a group of Italians arrived from Sorrento—Rosanna, Attilio, Mariano and Loredana. It was their first visit not only to Ananda, but to the United States. In Sorrento the year before, Swami had met all four of them, and their group PEKI, and had felt a strong connection with what they were doing spiritually. Working with a Catholic priest, Padre Luigi, members of the group were exploring their unique relationship with the Catholic Church.

Swami's meeting with PEKI marked the beginning of an ongoing exchange of energy, ideas, music and people between Ananda in America and Ananda in Italy. Although the connection with PEKI did not continue, the connection with Italy, and eventually with all of Europe, did. Swami felt that the consciousness and vibration coming from Italy would be helpful to the overall development of Ananda. The Italians were fun, and more outgoing in their expression than we were at Ananda Village. They quite naturally included children in their spiritual events and lives, a relaxed attitude that helped bring a needed shift in our expression of the spiritual life.

It was in 1984, with the arrival of Ram and Dianna, Prahlad and Keshava, that Ananda's work in Italy and Europe began to take shape. These four Swami had invited to Italy to see what might be possible. When Dianna asked Swami how she should look at her time in Italy, he responded, "Look at it as a nice vacation." What he was saying was, if things don't work out, you can simply go home. But if they do work out, then you will likely be living in Italy for some time. Things *did* work out, and in a big way; Ram and Dianna ended up being the spiritual directors of our newly established work in Italy and Europe for the following seven and a half years.

The early years of Ananda's work in Italy and Europe found creative expression in music that came through Swami. His visit to Assisi led to music for a St. Francis slide show; a visit to Italy's Amalfi coast inspired the music for Mediterranean Magic. The Different Worlds slideshow and the music Swami wrote for it were inspired by photos he had taken around the world of people of all ages, their faces reflecting the states of consciousness they had attained in their lives.

Early in 1983, Swami invited a group of us to join him weekly at his dome—Jyotish and Devi, David and Asha, Puru and Kirtani, Shivani, Seva, and myself. This was Swami's way of gathering together a group of friends (as he put it) with whom he could talk things over in an informal way. After the initial group dissolved, in early fall of 1983, Swami invited a group to Hawaii—Jyotish and Devi, David and Asha, Hriman and Padma, Seva, Arjuna and Shivani, and Durga and Vidura. These gatherings, I think, gave Swami a way to gauge the dynamics among people he saw as future leaders of Ananda.

Atherton Center (1983–1985)

A new adventure was also about to begin in my life. Earlier in the fall of 1983 we received word that Jerry Haslam, who had started the Atherton Center in 1980, was ready to move on. The single-story house in Atherton served not only for Sunday Services, classes, and events, but also allowed the seventeen ashram residents to share a spiritual lifestyle similar to that of San Francisco's Ananda House.

In the fall, before he left for the Holy Land, Swami was trying to feel who could be Jerry's replacement. He needed to consider the nature of the area, Atherton-Palo Alto, home to our East West Bookshop, with its intellectually sophisticated audience. We all puzzled over the right choice. Swami thought of Santosh and Valerie, or possibly Asha, but none of these was quite the right fit at that time. Then, turning to me, he said, "Parvati, maybe you can go there." I said I would be happy to go, knowing, as of course Swami himself did, that it wasn't really the ideal place for me—but knowing also that someone needed to go simply to keep the center going.

When Swami returned from a trip to the Holy Land that fall, I felt him withdraw his energy from me, particularly in my role as his secretary. Though it was not an easy time for me, I knew it was time for a change; I knew, and of course Swami knew, it was time for me to change gears. Suddenly, Keshava was once again his secretary, and I was not! And Swami no longer related to me in that role. Though our first meeting at Ananda House on his return from the Holy Land was awkward for me, I knew I needed to make the transition and prepare for my new adventure in Atherton. I would again be moving away from Ananda Village, leaving Swami and all my friends. My naturally even-minded temperament understood this reality. I knew the change needed to take place, and I was ready. Though times of transition can be a little shaky, I simply packed up my things at Ayodhya and moved to Atherton.

Living in the Atherton House was quite a change from San Francisco. It was a one-story summer bungalow (built decades earlier) with a swimming pool in the back, a pool house, and a cottage. The house itself did not have any elegance, but it did have a sweet feel. And since all the homes in the exclusive area of Atherton are required to be on at least one acre of land, this one too had a pleasant, if somewhat unkempt, yard around it.

Because I made the move to Atherton in December 1983, Christmas and Master's birthday were the first events of my time there.

During my first few months at the Atherton house, I lived there alone with the seventeen ashram residents. When I told Swami I needed help running the Center, he thought I would be all right on my own for a while. I disagreed, and asked for Bharat and Anandi, who had just finished building their house at the Village. It was a source of wry amusement in those days that no sooner did someone finish building a home, that they then would be asked to go out to one of the centers! We saw the pattern as Divine Mother's little joke — Her way of keeping us non-attached to what we were doing.

Bharat and Anandi did come, and the three of us directed the center in Atherton until I left in March 1985. My time there was the mix I had expected, challenging but also enjoyable.

Christ Lives Oratorio (1983–1984)

After the Hawaii trip in the fall of 1983, Swami and Rosanna traveled together to the Holy Land. Swami was deeply inspired by being there, especially being there with Rosanna, and by what he felt in meditation at the holy places associated with the life of

Christ. It was at this time that he wrote the music for the *Christ Lives Oratorio*. When in late fall he returned to Ananda House in San Francisco, I drove down from the Village to meet him. I was just nearing the end of my time acting as his secretary. As he came downstairs the next morning carrying a *very small* Casio keyboard, Swami said, "I've just composed wonderful songs about the life of Jesus." He began playing them on the Casio, but I really couldn't tell what they sounded like! Swami was deeply inspired and we, his listeners, were all looking a little perplexed—Bent, myself, Ram and Dianna, and others there. When Swami returned to Ananda Village, he immediately began composing arrangements for the music that had come to him. By the beginning of 1984, some arrangements already completed, and not wanting to lose momentum, he began recording what was to become the beautiful *Christ Lives Oratorio*. More arrangements followed and their recordings, many involving a full choir, all of it completed during the early months of 1984.

It was a massive undertaking, and deeply inspiring, not only for Swami but for all those involved in singing and recording. From my new home in Atherton, I had no direct connection with this project, but was well aware of his absorption in it. Even at a distance, the intensity and deep inspiration of Swami's energy was palpable. Knowing as he did that other critical needs might intervene at any time, Swami pushed right through into recording as soon as he was satisfied with the composing.

The recording complete, Swami arranged to have the *Christ Lives Oratorio* performed at all the locations available to him, including each of the Ananda centers. We could feel how deeply inspired Swami himself was by the music that had come through him. Through this music, I understood on a deep, vibrational level, and for the first time, the true meaning of the life of Jesus. That spring, at the ashram house in Atherton, recordings of the *Oratorio* music were played continuously by those living there, providing deep and enduring inspiration—an expression of the high consciousness that pervaded that time.

A Spiritual Healing

I had intended to be at every Oratorio performance — Roseville, Sacramento, Walnut Creek, San Francisco, and Atherton/Menlo Park — especially because Swami himself would be performing. Unfortunately, during this entire time, and though I very rarely became unwell, I found myself flat on my back in bed and feeling quite ill with the flu. I was so sick that I was only able to make it to the final performance that took place in Menlo Park. It was a strange experience for me. I felt terrible not being able to attend the performances! But this story has a happy ending.

When Swami arrived at the Atherton house before that final performance, he stayed in the little cottage we had prepared for him in back of the main house. My thought at the time was, "I don't care if I'm on my death bed, I am going to this performance tonight! I will not miss all of them." When I asked to ride with Swami to the performance, my wish was granted. The evening was for me deeply inspiring, spiritually thrilling.

The next morning, we all drove to the San Francisco airport to see Swami off. He was flying to Italy that very day, to start what was to become Ananda's work in Italy and Europe. Suddenly Swami was gone! For those of us who remained behind, Swami's departure felt as strange as if, after so beautifully writing the life of Jesus in the language of music, he had left for another planet.

My personal experience that day was of spiritual healing. Outwardly, I simply got up early and drove off to the airport. After Swami's departure, the day included a number of meetings to deal with the effects of Swami being away for quite some time. (As it turned out, he was away several months.) The day was so busy that only in the afternoon did I realize I wasn't sick anymore. Not at all unwell. I felt I had been healed by Swami — simply by being absorbed in the deep spiritual vibration coming through his music. He had not said anything to me. There was no outward show. Now up and about, I felt wonderful! Here was true proof to me of how spiritual healing works — the process cannot be explained rationally, yet is undeniably real. The healing, I realized, was spiritual in nature; my part lay in being open and attuned to its presence.

Swami departed for Italy in the beginning of February, Ram and Dianna in the beginning of March, and Keshava and Prahlad soon after. And so began Ananda's work in Italy and Europe.

1984 was a year of frequent travel for me. Based in Atherton with Bharat and Anandi, I drove between Atherton and Ananda House in San Francisco, helping to oversee both of these centers. I did a lot of driving in that year, including an occasional trip to the Village. The energy of the year was thrilling for me. The spiritual inspiration I felt was partly from the *Oratorio*, and partly from my connection with Ram and Dianna in Italy, and through them, with the expansion of Ananda's work there. Much as I missed these friends in a personal way, it was through them that I felt the inspiration of all that was happening in Italy.

Lawsuits (1984)

 *When boisterous storms of trials shriek,*
And when worries howl at me,
I will drown their noises, loudly chanting:
God! God! God!

Part of my 1984 adventure was a first exposure to lawsuits. Both the Atherton House and the San Francisco Ananda House were sued by their respective cities. In our Atherton House newsletter, we had advertised a guest house for our congregation. A letter soon came from the city saying, effectively, "Don't you know you can't do this, and we'll sue you if you do." When I wrote back to apologize and promise not to have a guest house, that threat faded away.

In San Francisco the story played out differently. From the time Ananda first moved into Ananda House in 1979, our next-door neighbor, often referred to as the "Teddy Bear" man — teddy bears were placed in all windows of his house — tried to have us evicted. He didn't like us being there, didn't like what we were doing, and from the beginning had threatened to sue. He was well aware that we were a substantial number living together in the middle of a very exclusive residential neighborhood. By 1984, talking with our neighbors and with the city of San Francisco, he thought he had gathered enough momentum to actually sue us. Zach Stewart, Bent, and I spent most of that year trying to avoid an actual legal confrontation.

Zach, an architect and a friend, had lived in San Francisco for decades. Because of his professional relationship with many of the officials in the planning department, he had developed strategies for working with them, strategies that came in very handy at this time. The city of San Francisco had issued a "shotgun" lawsuit, directed against every person individually that lived in Ananda House, including Jyotish and Devi, Swami, and many others who no longer lived there. The names were gathered from applications with our address for parking permits. The lawsuit was naturally intimidating to our residents, as of course it was meant to be. Bent and I worked closely together that year fending off the lawsuit in the "non-direct" way recommended by Zach. A tremendous amount of our energy went into simply trying to save the house as a home for our residents. By the end of the year, we had won through to victory. Our landlady and her lawyer were persuaded to take our side against the city. Without their support, the city couldn't pursue its legal action. We were fortunate not to face a legal battle in court; we simply did not have the financial means to do so. By November 1984, the threat of legal action had diminished enough to no longer be a concern. Little by little, in indirect ways, following Zach's invaluable guidance, we were able to show the City that they didn't have a case against us. The City backed off and dropped the case. We were deeply grateful to Zach, as we could not have won through without his guidance and help.

I should mention that at one point our landlady's lawyer began siding with the City on her behalf. I responded by calling her and letting her know that we would then have no option but to move out immediately. Then Swami, hearing about this, called our landlady directly. He simply asked her, "Do you want us in your house?"

This was the right question. When she answered, "Yes," the energy changed completely. I certainly learned a lot working on this lawsuit. Although I was on fire to deal with it at the time, and enjoyed the challenge, I was very glad when it was over!

From Monastic Calling to Spiritual Relationship

Toward the end of 1984 a major change came into my life through working with Bent. While I was living in the Atherton Center, we began teaching classes together, a shared service we both enjoyed. I was at the end of ten years as a nun and felt something new coming. He, at the same time, was coming to the end of a marriage. Working together, especially in teaching the Yoga Teacher Training Course, we had become good friends. By the beginning of 1985 we were exploring a relationship.

Lake Como, Italy (1985)

On Master's Birthday, 1985, Swami asked me if I would like to move to Italy. Though I had long wanted to do so, my newly developing relationship left me feeling torn. It was a moment in time — a moment to choose my next step. My decision in the end was to go to Italy; in March of that year, I made the journey. For several reasons Italy felt like the right step: I knew that our relationship needed time and space to develop in the right way; and I felt a need to experience living in Italy and Europe on my own, but with Ananda and Swami as my home base.

There were four of us on the flight to Europe that March — myself, Kirtani, Mayadevi Lauer, and Karin von Zieglauer (later Levin, when she married Danny Levin in 1987). Kirtani and I were on our way to Lake Como and Ananda's developing work there; Mayadevi and Karin were on their way to visit family in Germany and northern Italy, respectively.

Moving to Italy was a wonderful adventure for me — not destined to last long, but wonderful nonetheless. I had for many years wanted to live in Europe and felt it was part of my karma to do so. Kirtani and I lived in the newly established Ananda Center outside Como, in the tiny village of Veglio, located in the Val'di Intelvi. When we arrived in mid-March 1985, Jyotish and Devi had been there nine months, since the fall of 1984. Ram and Dianna had been in Italy for about a year. Jyotish, Devi, Ram, and Dianna as well as Patricia London, Lila Devi, Judy Fox, and a few others—had just come through a long, and extremely cold, winter, and had done so in an essentially unheated summer villa in the mountains! Located near the Swiss border and the city of Lugano, an area accustomed to deep snow in winter, the villa experienced a record snowfall in the winter of 1984–85. It was one of Europe's coldest winters in a century. With four to five feet of snow on the ground, no guests were able to come; with no income from paying guests, and little money to meet expenses, the residents struggled through the winter.

When Kirtani and I arrived, we heard the tale of how they survived that winter together and what they learned in the process. It had been quite an adventure. But now life at the villa was moving forward. Spring brought milder weather; Easter was only a few weeks away. When Swami arrived not long after Kirtani and I, he brought with him a whole new energy. It was wonderful to see how he related to the Italians, to hear him lecture in Italian, and to hear the stories that were so familiar to us but in a new language. Though no Italians actually lived with us at the Villa Rombolotti, they did come to visit; among them was Alessandra Buonsignore. It was her family's summer home we were renting, and Alessandra visited periodically from her home in Milan.

It was magical to be with Swami in Italy. Taking us with him, showing us the sights, Swami introduced us to the country. It was a very sweet time on a mundane as well as on a spiritual level. That spring Kirtani and I visited Assisi and Florence on our own. Weeks later we went with Swami to Rome, and on to southern Italy for programs he was giving there. In Rome, we visited Contessa Renata Arlini at her home. Swami had Kirtani and me sing for her *Father,*

Now that I Wander with Thee while he translated each of the verses into Italian. Renata had known Swami since his SRF days, when he toured Italy and Europe; she had a deep respect for and spiritual understanding of who Swami was. She took us on a day trip to Rieti, located near Greccio, to be in the presence of relics of St. Francis, and on the site of his painful eye treatment (a hot iron applied to his temples). It was at Rieti that St. Francis had a vision of Christ and received The Rule for the Friars Minor. After we meditated with Swami in the cave/grotto where this vision took place, Swami blessed each one there individually.

We then traveled to southern Italy, to the town of Catanzaro, located in the Calabria region. The Italians there were quite different from those we had met so far. During meals, the devotees there were perfectly at ease playing guitar, smoking, and drinking wine. And there was Swami, in the midst of all this, calmly sharing the spiritual teachings. It was an eye-opener for me. For part of the time in southern Italy, Rosanna joined us; she and Swami had arranged to see Natuzza, a well-known psychic living in the area.

From southern Italy, Kirtani and I traveled with Swami by train to Napoli, then (thanks to a thoughtful gift from Patricia London) by ferry to the island of Capri. For two nights Kirtani and I stayed in the same hotel as Swami. She and I had a lovely room with a view overlooking the ocean below. Rosanna visited Swami here; on one occasion we saw them strolling down one of Capri's picturesque streets. It was at this time, June 1985, that he and Rosanna were deciding if and when they would marry.

On our visit to Capri Swami told us, "You *have* to go and see the Blue Grotto [Grotta Azzura]. It's one of the seven wonders of the world!" As a young boy, sometime in the 1930s, Swami had been there with his parents; he had always remembered its beauty. And so down Kirtani and I went to the harbor to board a boat to take us to the Grotta. The boat we boarded was fairly large, but, unknown to us, one that could not actually enter the Grotta. In mid-ocean, just outside the Grotta entrance, and assisted by highly skilled seamen — I don't think they drop many passengers into the water!—we transferred to a *much* smaller boat that held three or four people. The seaman piloting this boat, approached the entrance, grabbed a large chain fastened to the roof, and, poof, we were inside! The color of the water inside the Grotta is truly amazing: a deep, crystal-clear blue found nowhere else. Taking advantage of this special moment in time, Kirtani and I said to the boatman, "Vorremo nuatare." We would like to swim. And, though swimming is not usually allowed, he actually let us climb out of the boat and swim! Divine Mother made an exception for us. In the water we sang Swami's song, "swim in the blue grotto, silver on your skin." It was a sweet and delightful time.

Together with Swami, we visited the Capri studio and shop of the painter, Guido Odierna. Swami bought small Odierna paintings for Kirtani and me—early birthday gifts, he said, since our birthdays were not until August. Swami's sweet and thoughtful gift hangs on our living room wall, a fond memory of a lovely time with him.

From Capri, Kirtani and I traveled with Swami by train from Naples to Florence, on to Milan, and then to the Como train station. Ram, Dianna, and Keshava had already returned to Como by car. On our long train ride, when we shared a meal with Swami in the dining car, once again he paid for all of us. When I said, in a humorous way, "Some friends we are!" Swami looked at us both very sweetly and said, "I am very lucky to have such friends as you."

We learned a lot from seeing how Swami related to the many different kinds of people we met in Italy. Hearing him lecture many times in Italian helped us learn the language—especially when we heard the same spiritual stories we had so often heard in English. We were especially aware of the strongly devotional—and emotional!—nature of Italy and the Italians—so different from the American vibration we had grown up with. We found ourselves laughing a lot, with good-humored awareness of our beginning understanding of the language and culture of Italy.

I am very appreciative of my experience at the Ananda Como center. Being in Italy was important for me vibrationally and spiritually and helped me to attune to a different consciousness and rhythm of life.

It was also during my stay in Como that I had the opportunity to visit Assisi for the first time. Kirtani, Karin, and I drove down with Jyotish and Devi, who were taking a little time for themselves before moving back to America. It turned out to be a very special trip for me. We arrived in Assisi in early May, right after the annual Calendimaggio festival. The flags from the festival were still flying in the streets, but (rare in Assisi) few people were to be seen. Though this was my first visit to Assisi, it somehow felt familiar as I walked the streets of the town.

In Assisi, the three of us stayed in an inexpensive pensione just outside the city gates. Each day we walked in to go to the many pilgrimage places associated with the life of St. Francis. For me this small city had a sweet and magical feeling. We sang Swami's songs in the Basilica of Santa Chiara (St. Clare), where her body is on display. It was early in the morning when Kirtani, Karin and I sang "Lord Most High" in memory of Clare and all that had happened in her lifetime with St. Francis. We meditated in the Basilica's Chapel seated before the original cross that spoke to Francis. At San Damiano we meditated and sang in the open room where St. Clare and her sister nuns slept. The pervasive vibration of our time in Assisi was sweet and familiar. I felt that I and others had lived in Assisi in Clare's time — that at Ananda we were living similar lives of simplicity and total dedication to God through our path of Self-realization, through our attunement to Swami and Master.

The Quiet Fall of 1985 at Como

That fall at the Villa Rombolotti was *very* quiet. Ram and Dianna were to leave in September for their first visit to America in a year and a half. Before their departure, a group of us traveled down to Sorrento for a wedding in a large Catholic church, a journey that was fun for us and a welcome mini vacation. As we returned to Como, Ram and Dianna left us at the Assisi train station to begin their journey back to America (by train to Rome, and then by plane to San Francisco).

Because Swami, together with Jyotish and Devi, had already left Como in June, by late September only Kirtani and I and a few others remained at Villa Rombolotti. In October our van (and only vehicle) was confiscated by the Italian Carabinieri at the Dogana (border crossing) into Switzerland. Because we had never been able to properly register this vehicle in Italy, we were well aware that the van could be taken at any time. Still, it was a shock to realize how completely on our own we now were—and with no car! To buy food, we now had to travel by bus into Como, a 45-minute ride each way, carrying in bags whatever groceries we needed, both for ourselves and for any guests we might have. Our only guest for several weeks that fall was Elisabeth, a woman visiting from Sweden. We were very happy she had come. Elisabeth later moved to Ananda Village where, in time, she was married to Binay, and was given the spiritual name Lina (absorbed or united)!

Kirtani and I knew change would come in November. All we had to do was hang on until then. The large pilgrimage group from Ananda travelling in the Holy Land with Swami and Rosanna would end their pilgrimage by visiting Assisi and then come to stay with us at Como. Fresh from their blessed pilgrimage, inspired by singing Oratorio songs written by Swami just the year before, their arrival would end our time of isolation.

In early November, Bent joined me in Como, and together we traveled to Assisi to arrange housing for the arriving group. It was quite a scene when the large group of more than fifty Americans arrived in Assisi—and we were so very glad to see them all!

It was a wonderful time for all of us to be together—the pilgrimage group, our Como group, and Swami and Rosanna. We brought the pilgrims by bus to Como and to the Villa in the very small village of Veglio. Because the tour buses were too large to drive all the way up to the Villa, we unloaded people and luggage in the snow (it was, after all, November and quite cold), and walked up the hill to the Villa! The luggage came behind in smaller vehicles.

Swami's presence, and this special pilgrimage, dramatically broke open the energy for the beginning of our work in Italy. From this time on Ananda's energy moved forward more smoothly. Several years later Ananda's work moved to the Assisi area and found its permanent location there in 1987. As Swami often mentioned to us, the tapasya of those early years was necessary. Those who were willing and able to take part in it gained spiritually; we learned valuable lessons about courage, faith, determination, will power, and, most of all, about trusting in Master and Divine Mother when everything was looking a little bleak. It was a great adventure then, and continues to be so now. I feel blessed to have been a part of it.

It was also during the fall of 1985 that Shivani and Arjuna arrived at Villa Rombolotti. Swami had asked them to move to Italy and help with the work there, and they had said yes. I always remember with amazement the evening Shivani arrived at the Villa. She came before Arjuna with two *completely full taxis* containing their luggage as well as a number of computers. Both taxis were absolutely stuffed! Because in those years computer equipment was very expensive to buy in Europe, it was essential to bring what was needed from America. Shivani and Arjuna have continued to live and serve in Italy and throughout Europe; they have been instrumental in founding Ananda's European work.

A few months before the Holy Land pilgrimage, September 1985, in a beautiful ceremony attended by hundreds of people, Swami and Rosanna were married at Crystal Hermitage. It was on this occasion that the Ananda wedding ceremony and music, recently written by Swami, was first introduced. The wedding was a momentous time for Ananda! And, to our regret, neither Kirtani nor I were able to be there!

I spent nine months in Italy at Lake Como. Once a week Bent and I spoke by phone as our relationship continued to evolve. Finally, in the beginning of November 1985, Bent arrived in Como, in time to serve with me when the pilgrimage group arrived. In December, we returned to America together. Eight months later we were married.

We Return to Ananda Village (1986)

Back in Ananda Village, Bent and I lived in our house at Ayodhya; beginning in January 1986, we served in directing the Ananda Spiritual Family, Ananda's outreach ministry. Our office, like all the offices for ministerial functions, was in the Publications building (now Hansa temple). Also in the building were Catherine Kairavi, who had established the Fundraising Department in 1984; Ananda Publications; and many other areas of Ananda's outreach. Once again, we were not to remain long in the Village.

Our Wedding (August 16, 1986)

Our wedding was astral; the entire day had a wonderful feel — hot and somewhat humid, with clouds that turned the sky beautiful shades of pink and purple as the sun set.

On the terrace by the pool at Crystal Hermitage, we were married by Swami and Rosanna. The entire community, and my parents, attended the ceremony. To express the sacredness of spiritual marriage, Swami had created the words and music for this beautiful ceremony the year before for his own wedding to Rosanna. To complete the day, Roy and Paula had created a wedding cake that combined cake and profiteroles, an Italian specialty!

A number of years later, we discovered that the day we were married was the hundred-year anniversary of Ramakrishna's mahasamadhi — a touching addition to the special blessings we already felt.

My parents, hosted by Arati, spent the night after the wedding in our house at Ayodhya. Bent and I had left immediately after the wedding for a week-long honeymoon — the first night at the Ananda House in San Francisco, and then on to Santa Barbara.

Our wedding marked a natural turning point in my life. From then on, Bent and I would be sharing the wonderful spiritual adventures still to come.

Ananda Seattle is Born (September 1986)

The month before our wedding, July 1986, Swami asked Bent and me, and Bill (Krishnadas) and Uma, to start a center in Seattle. We all said yes. Only a few weeks after our wedding, and a week after the end of Spiritual Renewal Week, in September 1986, we moved to Seattle. The year was interesting and challenging. Though it wasn't easy for the four of us to work together — each one had many years of serving Ananda and working with Swami in unique ways — we managed to establish a center location, to live together in a house that was also used for public events, and to host Swami and Rosanna on a visit. We all did our best to make our service there work.

Swami Introduces the Festival of Light (December 1986)

At Ananda Village later that fall, Swami introduced the Festival of Light ceremony. The inspiration had come to him earlier that year, during his time at Ananda Assisi. Though the four of us had been in Seattle only since September, Swami asked us to return to Ananda Village when he introduced the Festival. We drove the entire 800 miles from Seattle to the Village in one day. We knew the first celebration was an important time to be with him. He performed the ceremony in the Chapel at the Hermitage packed with ministers. It was a deeply inspiring moment in time. On the same day Swami ordained the first Lightbearers, the four of us from Seattle among them. With the Festival came a dramatic change in Sunday Services. There were, as can be imagined, varying reactions to this change. To set the tone, and because the ceremony was so new and different, we offered the Festival every day at our newly established Center in Seattle. We sang all the songs a'cappella (without accompaniment). Except for during the weekly Sunday Service, few attended our daily Festivals.

Mother Hamilton

During the time Bent and I were in Seattle, we met Mildred Hamilton (Mother Hamilton), a direct disciple of Paramhansa Yogananda. A strong-willed individual, she had been the SRF Seattle Center leader during Master's lifetime. After his mahasamadhi, I believe she left SRF and traveled to India looking for a guru in the body; the one she found she followed for a time after her return from India. In her early 80s when we met her, and unable to speak well because of a stroke, she nonetheless, within the first few minutes of our sitting down with her, taught us both the Hong Sau and Om techniques. After she told us a little about her life, I asked her if she knew Brother Kriyananda. Her emphatic reply: "Yes, and I regret the day I ever heard that name!" When she knew him, Swami was in charge of the SRF Centers and was responsible for interacting with the Center leaders after Master passed. It was at a time when SRF was focusing on center activity. Swami told us that at this point some center leaders weren't even sharing Master's teachings. On hearing Mildred Hamilton's words about him, Swami said, "It's too bad she hasn't learned the most important lesson, compassion." During our meeting with Mother Hamilton, I could feel spiritual strength, but not depth. After her many years leading a center in Seattle, she now lived in an apartment and was cared for by a few of her followers.

Bent and I were in Seattle from September 1986 to September 1987, and moved back to the Village that same fall. Seattle continued to develop under the leadership of Purushottama and Lakshmi, serving together with Bill and Uma. In 1987 an ashram house was established. The present-day community began in 1990 with an apartment complex in the Lynnwood, Washington area.

Years At Ananda Village (1987–1989)

A Listening to Nature Pilgrimage (May 1988)

Back at Ananda Village in the fall of 1987, we again lived in the Ayodhya cluster. That winter I worked for Padma McGilloway at JAPA (Joyful Arts Production Association) in a small office building near Crystal Hermitage. My task was to organize the first (and only) Listening to Nature pilgrimage, led by Bharat and Anandi in May 1988. I was happy to be able to go on the pilgrimage myself, to play a support role while having a wonderful time with the pilgrims — among them Vidura, Paul Green, Babsi and her mother Helga, William Rowley, Tom Shott, and Shinichi from Japan.

We visited the south rim of the Grand Canyon (where we hiked half-way down the canyon), Bryce National Park, and Zion National Park, our last stop. Our itinerary formed a loop beginning and ending in Las Vegas, Nevada, a location convenient for air travel and for renting the vans needed for the pilgrimage. My brief description of each location: Zion is other-worldly; Bryce is a fairyland; and the Grand Canyon is majestic, ancient, and impersonal — each beautiful in a unique way.

A Cities of Light Program (Summer 1988)

In the summer of 1988, Bent and I developed and directed what we called a *Cities of Light* program. The purpose was to give an experience of living a spiritual life on a daily basis — more specifically, doing so at Ananda Village. The program was based at The Expanding Light and operated from May through September 1988. We had a total of sixty-five adults and twelve children — people of all ages (one woman in her seventies, Jacqueline Roulet, was a long-time SRF member from San Diego), families with children, single people, and couples. Dambara Begley stayed the whole summer. The focus was on *sadhana*, service, and *satsang* — a living experience of Ananda. Single people camped near The Expanding Light; families camped near the farmhouse on Tyler Foote Road.

When we were planning the program Jaya Helin made a memorable comment—he saw the people in the program:

Working hard

Contributing something to the community

Deepening their spiritual life

And having fun!

To include these four elements, we did projects in various areas of the community, serving alongside community members. Areas included were Village maintenance, the Meditation Retreat, and Crystal Hermitage. Three hours of karma yoga each morning; two hours in the afternoon. Daily sadhanas, 6:00–8:00 am and 4:30–6:30 pm, included energization exercises, yoga postures, chanting, and 45 minutes of meditation. To honor the special nature of the *Cities of Light* program, we held our sadhanas separately from The Expanding Light's. We gave people lots of support to help them enjoy a longer meditation while letting them know they could leave quietly if they needed to.

At the beginning of each service project, we gave classes on Karma Yoga. At the beginning of each two-week segment of the program, we devoted time to orienting new people to Ananda as a whole. We wanted the participants to know what to expect—especially the nature of our spiritual path and its ceremonies. We taught or reviewed meditation, *Hong-Sau*, and the energization exercises. On Fridays after lunch, we began with a healing prayer circle, then, remembering Jaya's fourth point, switched to a fun afternoon of swimming or other outings. By Friday afternoon, we found, people *needed* a time for relaxation and fun!

One morning at breakfast, we found one of our newer arrivals standing in the dining room weeping softly to herself. She explained her emotion to us: "Even the plants here have energy! It's all too much for me." We suggested that she take the day off to relax and just enjoy the program as she felt to. From that time on she was better. She had simply needed time to adjust to the consciousness and vibration of Ananda—so much more alive than what she was used to. Today that same person is a core member of one of the Ananda communities, where she has been living since her time in the *Cities of Light* program.

Evening classes focused on Attunement, Raja Yoga, and Cities of Light (given by a number of Ananda teachers and exploring different aspects of Ananda). Weekends were free except for a two to three-hour period of service at The Expanding Light on either Saturday or Sunday. Meals were usually provided at The Expanding Light, with some lunches at Master's Market. It was a full and enjoyable schedule for most of those who attended. For those who found the schedule too full, we worked to help them find a fit.

A Book-Selling Trip for Crystal Clarity Publishers (Fall 1988)

In October 1988, we changed gears again, this time saying yes to a book-selling trip for Crystal Clarity Publishers. We flew to Boston to pick up the Ananda motorhome from Bob Rinzler and Lakshman Simpson, who had been selling books along the East coast. Driving north into New England, we visited Ananda devotees and sold books at many small bookstores throughout New England. Living in the motorhome as we traveled brought new adventures—selling to a Wicca bookstore in Salem, Massachusetts on Halloween day (they loved several of Swami's books!), and to stores in Newport, Rhode Island, where a video series on The Kennedys was being filmed. Along the way we learned to drop by the local police station when we needed to spend the night in a town and ask their advice about where to park—a practice that saved us a lot of trouble! A special blessing of motoring through New England in October was seeing the fall colors in their full glory.

Driving west from New England, we sold books and visited devotees in Chicago and Salt Lake City. In between, two flat tires on a Friday afternoon brought an unplanned weekend in Lincoln,

Nebraska! In Salt Lake City we offered programs together with Devi, then on to Ananda Village and home at last!

We Visit Amrit Desai's Kripalu Ashram

During our time in New England, we visited Amrit Desai's Kripalu Ashram in western Massachusetts. Given a tour of their very large facility, we learned that on weekends, their kitchens fed as many as five hundred guests. (We felt for their poor karma yogis!). The evening program was a Guru Vandana (celebration of the guru), a devotional service during which, to the accompaniment of loud chanting, those present were individually blessed by Amrit Desai. The next morning, as sadhana ended, to our great surprise, we found ourselves in the middle of a fundraising event! In little over an hour more than one hundred thousand dollars was raised for a support fund for their monastic members. We hadn't experienced a sadhana/fundraising event quite like this ever before!

Honeymoon in Kauai — Two Years Late

In November we took a much-needed two-week vacation to the island of Kauai — finally, two years after our marriage, a real honeymoon! — lovingly financed by both sets of parents. It was our first visit to this lovely island, and a wonderfully relaxing and enjoyable experience.

The Expanding Light, Bookselling, and Touring the American Southwest (1988–1989)

When we returned from Kauai late November 1988 (to find snow at Ananda Village!), we began serving at The Expanding Light, but not for long. In January 1989, responding to the need for Prahlad and Giuliana to be on staff, we volunteered to go once again on a book-selling tour — this time to the San Francisco Bay Area. We were back living in the motorhome, with no clear idea what lay ahead!

The Southwest Tour (Spring 1989)

As it turned out, at the end of our bookselling tour we again returned to serving at The Expanding Light. Like many who worked closely with Swami's vision for Ananda, Bent and I were actively looking for ways to bring more income to The Expanding Light and to Crystal Clarity Publishers.

One idea was that of a teaching tour to help draw more guests to The Expanding Light. The tour we planned was for a large southwest loop — Salt Lake City, Ft. Collins, Denver, Colorado Springs, Sedona, Phoenix, and Tucson, places where Ananda programs had been successful before. The tour would also be a way for us to see another part of America and to meet devotees there.

Our Southwest tour began Easter Sunday, March 26, 1989. We left after Swami's inspiring service, sent on our way with loving hugs from both Swami and Rosanna. The night before, we attended an Easter concert — the Oratorio with full choir and with Swami reading the script as well as doing several of the solos. Just before the concert, I found Swami upstairs in The Expanding Light office going over the program. He said he would really like a foot massage, and could I find someone to give him one? I said I would do it for him myself. "Are you good?" he asked. I said yes. It was a wonderful blessing to serve him in this way, and hopefully the massage was good for him as well!

Swami's Superconscious Dream

On Good Friday of this same Easter weekend, Swami came into the temple and gave an inspiring talk, including an account of a dream that had come to him just that morning:

"I had a very interesting dream in the early hours of this morning. I was reciting a vow for someone else to repeat. It was a vow of intense dedication to God, something like, 'I dedicate myself ....' And all through this vow that was being recited, there was thunder in the background, all the time getting stronger and stronger. I began to think, wow, when we finish the vow what's going to happen? I don't remember what the words were anymore; they didn't remain in my mind — but something like, 'I dedicate my entire being, all that I am, all that I have, to God.' At that moment came a thunderclap a thousand times greater than the loudest thunderclap you've ever heard. And then, voom, suddenly, it seemed like the end of the world; it was as if a dam had burst, and a huge flood came pouring out. I could see houses and furniture going up like matchsticks and being swept away by a raging flood. It looked like it was the end of everything. I remember my consciousness being altogether here, at the point between the eyebrows. I was thinking, well I have given my life to God; it doesn't matter. I felt very calm throughout. It was then that I woke up. I didn't know if I was drowning or what. But something I thought about later was of interest too. I remembered that the person to whom I was giving this vow was either a prince or a king. It was as if the ruler, the government in our case, was dedicating itself to God in time to be in that consciousness before some great disaster. And the disaster wasn't to destroy the world. All I saw in my mind being destroyed were houses and furniture. As if, what man has done in this century will be destroyed. And it will be destroyed so that we can have a new birth in God. I think there was truth in that dream. I think that we are headed for a great purging, a great suffering. But if we have our minds here [at the point between the eyebrows], if we have our minds strongly in the thought of God, then we will find that nothing can touch us. Master said, 'you must stand unshaken amidst the crash of breaking worlds.' When we come onto the spiritual path, we very quickly see how it separates the men from the boys."

It was with Swami's words in mind that we left on our tour of the Southwest.

We drove up to Interstate 80 and out across the Nevada desert. We spent the night at a motel in Winnemucca, Nevada, and on Monday afternoon arrived in Salt Lake City. That evening, after we led the Attunement Ceremony for the group there, we spent the night with Paul and Barbara Green.

Here are some of the descriptions from the tour:

Ft. Collins, Colorado

The next morning, we were up bright and early for a fairly long drive across southern Wyoming, a very barren stretch along Interstate 80. We arrived in Fort Collins, Colorado that evening and stayed at the home of Dennis and Bailey Stenson and their children. They live a simple life in an old farmhouse on ten acres of land on which they do organic gardening. A number of years ago, they lived at Ananda Village for about a year, but had not made it back since. At their home we led a kirtan for a group of people they know and a few that were new, about fourteen people altogether. We also showed the Ananda slide show (*Cities of Light*). It struck me afterwards that no one came and talked with me about Ananda at the end of our presentation. Though people seemed to enjoy the chanting and the whole evening, my feeling was that this group was too shy and too involved in their own lives to be interested in the need for anything more.

The next day we explored the city of Fort Collins, a growing college town.

Denver, Colorado

Thursday, March 30: We drove to Denver, an hour and a half south of Ft. Collins, and stayed with Linda DeMoss. Linda came to many of our classes when we were in Denver three years ago. She was very sweet to us, supportive, and of all the people we stayed with she seemed the clearest about why we were there. She both drew from us and gave to us. We went on a short hike with her Friday morning and then took the afternoon to prepare for our Friday night free talk and slide show on *Cities of Light*, as well as for the Saturday seminar on "Awaken the Light Within You" (Bringing Divine Power into Your Life).

Denver is a large city with sprawling suburbs. We met very nice and sincere people there. An incongruity of this city is that for all the lifeless feel of suburbia, its large buildings have some of the most interesting architecture I have ever seen. Saturday after the seminar brought snow flurries — big flakes! Twenty-two attended the free lecture and six came to the seminar the following day.

Sunday and Monday nights we had well-attended programs in nearby Colorado Springs, an hour and a quarter south of Denver: on Sunday, thirteen in Manitou Springs; on Monday, nineteen in Colorado Springs. Though unfortunately we hadn't time to see much of this area, I liked what I did see. The people who came to the programs seemed sincere and interested. There is certainly an energy to build on in Colorado!

Northern New Mexico

We spent Monday night in a motel in Colorado Springs (circa 1940s, very clean and $21.50 for two!). The next morning, we got an early start. The southwest mountains and desert are lovely. We drove south through Colorado on Interstate 25; just after crossing the border into New Mexico, we cut off to go up through the mountains. We wanted to see Taos and the surrounding area. A beautiful drive with clear, good weather allowed us to really enjoy the scenery: high mountains and forests. We drove through Cimarron, Eagle's Nest, Taos, and Rancho de Taos. Taos itself is on a high desert-like plateau with mountains and forest all around. To get a feel for this quaint town of mostly adobe structures we took time to walk the streets. Many artists, ranchers, and Native Americans, and spiritually seeking people live in the area — quite a variety of energies. The town is a tourist attraction, but one with charm and energy. Twenty miles outside the town is the Lama Foundation, associated with Ram Dass. We had lunch at the local health food store in Taos, and then headed south to Santa Fe. Because the highway we followed goes along a portion of the Rio Grande we were treated to a good view of this well-known river.

Santa Fe was well worth seeing. Before continuing on to Albuquerque, we walked for an hour through the old downtown area. Santa Fe's adobe structures give it a wonderful southwest charm, uniquely in harmony with the surrounding landscape. We felt déjà vu in Santa Fe's town square, so exactly alike in design to the one in Sonoma, California, which we had visited several months before on our Crystal Clarity sales trip.

After our long day's scenic drive, we stayed the night in Albuquerque and enjoyed a wonderful swim, hot tub, and sauna. Wednesday, April 5, a day that turned out to be momentous, we left early (no sightseeing in this city) for our long drive to Sedona. We needed to get there early enough for at least a little preparation for our evening program! The drive through the high desert of New Mexico and Arizona was beautiful. Looking at our map, I was thinking how I would one day (but not now!) like to explore the Native American mesas and pueblos of that area.

Sedona, Arizona

Unfortunately, because we had dallied a bit too long here and there, we reached Flagstaff a little late in the day, leaving us still with a 45-minute drive to reach Sedona, where we were to give our evening program. A wrong turn doubled the distance we needed to drive to where we were staying. With little time before we needed to leave for our program, we agreed to do our best to fit in a shower, meditation, and preparation for the evening, and even, as courtesy required, time with our hostess. Then, just as we were hastily unloading, we discovered that we were an hour early! Arizona, unlike most of the country, had not gone on daylight savings time. We felt Divine Mother was playing a little joke on us! And, as we were to see, Her jokes for the day weren't over. For the moment, though, we were able to relax with our host Joy Pollack, and still have time to get ready for the program.

Thirty-three people came that evening for an introductory talk and slide show on Cities of Light. Bent did a very good job presenting an overview of the ideal — that God is vital to Cities of Light, which are so much more than a social experiment. I felt that people were touched.

A Message from Ananda: "How's Your Italian?"

We arrived home at 9:30 pm to find a message on Joy's answering machine asking us to call Terry McGilloway, our boss at The Expanding Light, as soon as possible. Late as it was, we called and got through. As it turned out Terry was calling on behalf of Swami. Terry's first question to us was, "How's your Italian?"

Swami wanted to know how we felt about moving indefinitely to our center at Ananda Assisi, Italy to help out there! It was mind-boggling! Here we were in the middle of Arizona, all our energy going in the direction of our tour, and we were being asked to turn in a completely different direction. It is at such a time that the practice of yoga and our teachings becomes evident. I, of course, was very happy at the prospect. What an unexpected pleasure to be asked to go back to Italy! I had only recently given to Divine Mother my small but persistent desire to return there: "What I want is God and You. Wherever I am with You, is where I want to be." My response to Terry was an unequivocal Yes! I would love to go. But I told Terry, he should talk with Bent directly, as I wasn't sure what his response would be. Doing my best to put aside my desires, I waited for Bent to absorb Swami's request. His response too was, yes! He agreed with some hesitation in his heart (as he put it), for language is not his strong point. We called Swami the next morning; Bent told him we were both enthusiastic about moving to Italy and helping our work there.

Joy, our host, witnessing our dramatic phone conversations, realized with some amazement that she was the first to hear the news and to see how we were handling our new direction. I didn't sleep much that night. The excitement was just too much!

The next day the three of us went for a day's adventure to the Grand Canyon, which neither she nor Bent had visited. After our news of the night before, this outing was the perfect way to channel all that energy! In the morning, we drove up to the South Rim, two hours north of Sedona. Just outside the park, at the Imax theater, we viewed their amazing presentation of the Grand

Canyon. The screen is five-stories high with speakers all around. Viewers feel themselves flying through the canyon skimming the waters of the Colorado River. We were all holding on to our seats! On our way to the South Rim, we stopped at several points for magnificent views of the canyon. I had visited this wonder of the world four times in the previous four years, three times in the last year and a half. It felt good to see it again; by now I felt I was visiting an old friend. The Grand Canyon—vast and impersonal—representative in a way of the feeling and spirit of America. Eating sandwiches, we drove all along the South Rim thrilled by the beautiful sights. In the evening of this delightful day, we drove out through the Navajo reservation and back down into Flagstaff and Sedona.

Friday, April 7, we visited the woman sponsoring us for the Sedona programs; in the afternoon we studied for the following day's seminar. We were naturally disappointed when only three people out of the thirty-three from Wednesday evening showed up. The program itself went well, but we were trying to cover too much material. Like many first-time ventures, this one gave us food for thought—how in future to make the seminar work better. That afternoon we went to Red Rock Crossing, one of the most picturesque spots in Sedona, and waded in Oak Creek. The day was quite warm; and it felt great to be outside and in the water.

Phoenix, Arizona

The next day, Sunday, April 9, we drove early to Phoenix in time to attend an 11 am Church of Religious Science Sunday service. During the whole of our two-hour drive from Sedona to Phoenix, we enjoyed the glorious sight of the surrounding desert in bloom—ocotillo, prickly pear, saguaro—with all their colorful flowers. The sight made me very happy.

After the Sunday service, we made a good connection for the future with the very nice woman who directs special events for the Church. Our time in Phoenix was devoted mainly to making such contacts as well as to giving two small evening talks—one at a local bookstore and one at the ARE Clinic connected with Edgar Cayce. We also made connections with The Rim Institute (Jo Norris), The Franciscan Renewal Center (Pat Bried), and the Logos Center (Joe Dillard).

From Phoenix we went on to visit my parents in Palm Springs, and then drove up Hwy 99 and home to Ananda Village. We were happy with the attendance at our programs, and with the contacts we had made for future programs.

We arrived at Ananda just in time to say goodbye, early the following morning, to all those who were leaving on the second Pilgrimage to Master's Shrines with Swami. After so long on the road, it was sweet for us to see everyone, even if just to say goodbye. Bent went into seclusion that same afternoon, and I followed the next evening, both of us at the Seclusion Retreat.

A Test of Willingness

Our seclusion was not to last long. Swami felt we were needed in Assisi as soon as possible. Though we had said yes to this move, and meant it, the prospect of a direction so dramatically different from touring and working at The Expanding Light came as a shock. I felt as though I had been traveling very fast in a particular direction only to suddenly hit a brick wall. I found it hard at first to wrap my mind around this new idea. Though on one level I was thrilled to be asked to go to Italy, the idea had seemed so unlikely to happen that I had given it up. And now here it was! For Bent the idea was more challenging; he didn't have the desire I did to serve in Italy. Nonetheless, he too was willing and simply wanted to help out wherever Swami felt we were needed.

Swami wanted us to leave as soon as we could: "I don't want to strip your gears, but you are needed there as soon as you can go." The upshot was that, after a few days of seclusion, we began preparing for the move to Italy—selling our car and putting everything we owned in storage. When on May 15 we left with Shivani, we carried with us four very large suitcases containing what we would need for living and teaching in Italy. And so began another wild and wonderful adventure.

Ananda Assisi (May 1989–September 1990)

This time we were moving not to Como, but to Assisi. Our service there was to be a great blessing, but by no means easy! It was wonderful to be at the Ananda Retreat, near Assisi and in the vibration of St. Francis. Ram and Dianna, still living in Assisi and in charge of the work, had done a fine job beginning a work in a difficult situation—different country, language, customs, expectations. The center itself had moved twice before finally landing permanently at Il Rifugio, located in the countryside sixteen kilometers outside Assisi. The challenge for Ananda Assisi at this time was that so many energies were needed for Ananda's multifaceted work in Italy and Europe that those living there were being pulled out of balance.

A Need for Balance

At the time we arrived, there was *a lot* of outreach going on from Ananda Assisi! Our task was to try to help bring balance to these very dynamic energies. We were only mildly successful. There was so much touring and outreach going on!—teaching tours, business outreach, choir touring—but with no clear core, no central focus, and not enough grounding energy. The center was like a balloon expanding so far beyond its limits that we wondered when it would pop. The tremendously active outreach *did* very much need to happen. What was lacking was coordination from a center.

We did our best to blend into the existing energy, to help bring it to a grounded and workable state. Working in the office, we took reservations for the retreat, for the most part in Italian (which we were still learning)! We also helped out with the businesses, especially with the meditation cushions, made at Il Rifugio and sold all over Europe. I sang in the choir and helped with correspondence. Because so much needed to happen during those early years of establishing Ananda's work in Italy and Europe, the residents living at Ananda Assisi were serving in many different areas at the same time—choir tours, making and selling meditation cushions, teaching tours, housekeeping at the retreat, working with publications, working in the kitchen, and more. Areas of service seemed piled layer upon layer on the willing residents, but with a continuing challenge as to how to coordinate the overlapping demands.

Swami himself was trying to help stabilize and ground the energy. We all realized there was a problem when we heard the Italians were referring to the staff at Il Rifugio as the ragazzi (the kids). In trying to bring stability in this challenging time, Bent and I found ourselves in the middle of a whirlwind of activity.

For all the challenge, we enjoyed our time at Ananda Assisi, and in Italy generally. We took Italian lessons, enjoyed eating pizza and fresh mozzarella, and often visited Assisi itself, immersing ourselves in the town and its deeply spiritual vibrations. We made a friend of one of the friars at the Basilica of St. Francis, Padre Testa, originally from Australia, and therefore English-speaking. When one day, we greeted him warmly outside the Basilica of St. Francis, someone in his small Catholic tour group asked him, "Are these people Catholic?" His reply was very sweet and perceptive: "As you can see, the fingers on my hand that seem separate, are all part of my hand, these people are simply another finger on the hand of God."

The Spirit of St. Francis in Our Life at Ananda

I often felt, during our time in Italy, and especially in Assisi and the surrounding area, that we were living a present-day version of how St. Francis and his brothers had lived some eight hundred years earlier. What I read about St. Francis and his life with the monks, and about the nuns under St. Clare, felt familiar, very similar to how we were living at Ananda. The Friars Minor of that time lived happily with very few outward possessions. Similarly, our life at Ananda was inspired by Master's words about World Brotherhood Colonies: places where "simplicity of living and high thinking brings the greatest happiness." At Ananda Assisi we felt the joy of such simplicity and God-centered lives. Master had, in fact, called St. Francis his "patron saint." He brought St. Francis' teachings into the modern world when he said, "I prefer Lady simplicity to Lady poverty." Following in the footsteps of St. Francis, who was the first to start a third, or lay, order, Swami Kriyananda established a monastic order that included householders and married couples. Living where St. Francis and his monks had lived, we were immersed in his vibration. We felt especially close to Francis in Assisi, where he and his followers had brought forth in their time, as Ananda is doing in our time, a new understanding of monasticism and the spiritual life.

We also traveled! — to the island of Capri, to Florence and Rome, and — a special trip at the end of our time in Italy — to the monastery and church of Padre Pio in the Gargano region. We meditated in the church where he received the stigmata and toured his monastery home. We also visited the hospital, La Casa per La Solieva della Sofferenza (the house for the relief of suffering), that Padre Pio had built for the people of southern Italy. For many years it was the only hospital in that entire area. We also visited the nearby town of Monte Sant'Angelo. It happened to be the 1,500-year anniversary of a vision there of the Archangel Michael in 1490, who had manifested a crystal cross that year, and saved the town from a terrible plague raging in the area.

Everywhere in Italy are places associated with miracles and saints, so different from America — a difference especially strongly felt each time we travelled home to America from Italy. And travel home we did, after a little over a year in Assisi. We had let Swami and Rosanna know that it wasn't working for us to continue serving there. Mastering Italian had not been easy; but more to the point, we didn't feel we were having the needed effect of grounding the energy. That change did come eventually, but not until Swami himself moved to Assisi in 1997.

Ananda Village (1990–1992)

When we returned to the Village in September 1990, Bent went to work managing The Expanding Light. I worked briefly with the Kriya Ministry, and then also joined him on staff there. We decided to live at The Expanding Light in Friendship house; our experience in Ananda Assisi made living where we served especially appealing to us.

I now found myself, for the second time within a few years, experiencing the spiritual culture shock of moving from Italy to America. Italy is a country in which devotion to God is more easily expressed, and without embarrassment. America's more impersonal consciousness can allow one to more easily bypass emotion and go deeper into oneness with the Divine. Both of these are needed for spiritual growth, and Divine Mother was allowing me to experience this reality yet again.

Ananda In Texas (1992–1994)

Swami received such a tremendous response in Dallas, Texas in spring 1991 that he encouraged Ananda ministers to go to Texas more frequently. What began as monthly visits led to the suggestion of a several-month visit — to see if the time was right for a larger presence there, perhaps even a center. Because we were more available than other ministers, Bent volunteered us to make a three-month visit there.

During our initial visit, in January — April 1992, we spent a month at each of the Ananda meditation groups — Houston, Austin, and Dallas. We even spent a few days with the small group on South Padre Island. At the end of the three months, we held an all-Texas retreat outside Austin. At the end of the retreat, because the energy felt right, we asked those attending if they would like us to move there as the ministers for Texas. When the answer was positive, we asked everyone to pledge a monthly amount. We had to be sure the support for resident ministers was grounded in reality. With pledges totaling about $1,200/month, Bent and I felt we could try to make a go of it. We planned to move to Texas, with Austin as a home base, in August 1992.

Tapasya (austerity), in varying degrees of intensity, has always been part of any new Ananda undertaking. For our Texas adventure, the tapasya began even before we left Ananda Village!

The day we began our two-thousand-mile drive to Texas, as we pulled out from The Expanding Light parking lot in a large U-Haul van, our small automobile towed behind, we noticed frantic waving from the car behind us. Mistakenly assuming that the waving was a friendly farewell, we continued to the bottom of the hill before realizing that something was very wrong. We had forgotten to take the emergency brake off on the car. The car's rear tires, prevented from turning by the brake, were being shredded all the way down the driveway. Kind friends helped us remove the damaged tires, take them to Grass Valley for replacement, and bolt the new ones on—all within a few hours. Then, not missing a beat, we were finally on our way to Texas that same day!

With us in the U-Haul van was the altar that had for many years been in place at The Expanding Light temple and was just now being replaced. It was a blessing to be able to take this altar with us to its new Ananda home in Texas.

Nine-months into our time in Austin, we could see that there wasn't enough interest there for developing an Ananda center. Dallas, by contrast, did have this interest, and the group there urged us to come. In May 1993, we made the move, opened the Ananda Dallas Center in the Richardson area, and remained as ministers there until August 1994. In the summer of 1994, feeling the need for a change, Bent and I traded places with Krishnadas and Mantradevi, then living in Portland, Oregon.

Ananda Portland (1994—1995)

When we arrived at Portland, Oregon, Paula Lucki was the main minister, assisted by Kent and Marilyn Baughman, and by Daiva Glazzard—also briefly by Omprakash and Prem-Shanti Rider, until they were asked to move to Ananda Seattle in the fall.

The Portland Center went through many changes during our

sixteen-month stay: the restaurant on NW 23rd St. was expanded; a church location in the Beaverton area was purchased and development of it begun; and the search for a community location was begun to replace the NW 23rd St. ashram house sold the previous year.

By the time we arrived, the Song of the Rose Café, had moved and doubled in size. Still located in the same block of NW 23rd, the restaurant's new location was quickly losing money. In a staff of twenty-five, only a few Ananda people were employed there. The question was, "Why are we doing this?" In spring of 1995 we sold the restaurant; and at the same time, Paula finally found a community location to buy.

The first time I saw the new Ananda Portland community, it felt like a community. With a curved design, the apartments were located around a central lawn area. This central area contained a few more apartments and a swimming pool. The arrangement of living spaces and common areas was ideal. Our task now was to move a number of the previous residents out, move our Ananda members in, and start a community! As you can imagine, this transition meant years of ongoing hard work, as well as fun also. Such has been the story of each Ananda community.

We returned to Ananda Village from Portland at the end of December 1995. During the coming year Bent visited small bookstores all over the country selling books for Crystal Clarity. At first, I didn't know what I would do. Then, through a chance conversation with Vidura, in the beginning of 1996 I found myself living in the Ananda Palo Alto community and working on the lawsuit. These were years that were an extremely challenging time for Ananda.

The Lawsuit Years 1990–2002

Self-Realization Fellowship brought a lawsuit against Ananda in the fall of 1990. The scope of it was massive. As Jyotish and Devi Novak have written in the Preface to the book, *A Fight for Religious Freedom* by Jon R. Parsons:

.... in 1990 disaster struck again—this time not as a forest fire, but as a legal conflagration which threatened Ananda's existence more profoundly than any natural calamity. Self-Realization Fellowship, the organization founded by Paramhansa Yogananda in 1925, launched a complex and far-reaching legal attack against Ananda that ultimately lasted twelve years. The heart of their lawsuit, as the presiding judge, Edward Garcia, later observed was "to put Ananda out of business."

In 1990 SRF declared it had exclusive rights to the "territory" of Paramhansa Yogananda—his name, his image, his words, and his teachings. And, they were ready to wage war to maintain their control.

Ananda recognized, behind the mask of SRF's legal proceedings and papers, the face of suppression and control. And, the people of Ananda were ready to defend the principle of freedom, even to the point of putting their property and the life of Ananda at risk.

Ananda represented a new kind of spiritual organization. It too, was a monastic order, but one in which all members' points of view were heard and respected.

Despite the tremendous challenges of this initial lawsuit, by 1994 things were, from our perspective, progressing fairly well in Federal court. Many of the SRF lawsuit issues had been decided in Ananda's favor. We were now free to publish the original version of *Autobiography of a Yogi*; the term Self-realization had been declared generic (not owned by SRF!); Yogananda's name, image, likeness, and his teachings, were available for Ananda to use. We could move forward in sharing Master with people everywhere.

Now, however, a secondary sexual harassment lawsuit was launched against an Ananda minister and Swami Kriyananda that challenged our members and friends in a more personal way. Ananda members had to look at what they believed in and why. What was their direct experience of living at Ananda and with Swami? And did they have the courage to trust and stand up for that experience in the face of a battering and extremely negative energy? For many, the answer was yes. But everyone was tested. Standing firm in the midst of this swirling mass of energy was Swami Kriyananda, simply being himself. He never tried to defend *himself*; he was completely honest about who he was and what he had and had not done. I remember him saying to us, "I saw who you were when you came to Ananda, and I accepted you as you were. I expected that you would do the same for me."

While Bent toured the country selling books, I worked on the lawsuits, and also helped Catherine with Fundraising. Though I didn't feel either would be a long-term job for me, I saw that both areas needed help, and was glad to be able to serve in that way.

Ananda Portland (1998–2004)

After we left Ananda Portland in December 1995, Paula continued on as spiritual director for another six months. By spring of 1996, the cancer she had been dealing over the past few years had progressed to the point that she needed to move back to the Village. Kent and Marilyn Baughman (Hanuman and Mari) stepped in to lead Ananda Portland. When by the fall of 1997 it was clear to everyone involved that a change was needed, Jyotish and Devi asked us if we would be willing to return to Portland and direct the center and community there. Though the decision was not easy for us — our stay in Portland in 1994–95 had its difficulties — we understood that someone needed to go there, and that we were probably the best choice.

For the next six years, from the end of 1997 until the beginning of 2004, we served as spiritual directors of Ananda Portland. We moved to Portland just as the sexual harassment lawsuit was coming to a close, officially ending in February 1998 with a negative outcome for Ananda. The Ananda Church of Self-Realization, of Nevada County and Swami Kriyananda were fined well over a million dollars. Ananda stood on a precipice. We were under attack by rapacious lawyers trying to destroy us, even trying to take over the copyrights for Swami's books. Through a lot of hard work, and through Master's and Swami's grace, we came through this challenging time victorious.

The Power of Negativity

During the lawsuits, I was amazed to see how often people were ready to believe hearsay about happenings of which they had no direct experience. The negative energy directed at Ananda, and the magnetic field it created, sometimes had the power to overwhelm even the best of people.

In Portland, people who had been with us for some years and knew all of us personally, called to express their concern. In spite of many years of direct experience with us, a number of them took the 1998 legal judgement against Ananda and Swami as truth, and believed as true all the negative things said about us by a lawyer they had never met. It was a good lesson on the power of negativity. Neither Bent nor I experienced these doubts; we were very clear with people about how we felt and why.

We had regular satsangs to keep channels of communication open, to keep everyone informed about the progress of the lawsuit. We worked to raise money to help cover legal expenses and, after the final judgement, to pay off the enormous financial debt we had been forced to take on.

Beyond the lawsuit, our focus in Portland was to give energy to Community residents as well as to the Mandir and the congregation. The Community and Mandir are located about four miles apart, both in good areas of Portland and Beaverton. During our earlier stay, Bent and I lived in an upstairs apartment in the Mandir. On our return in 1998, we moved into an apartment in the middle of the Community. Keeping all the apartments rented — especially to devotees on our path — was our constant challenge. During our time there Ananda devotees made up around fifty percent of the Community population. Among others who lived there, some had no connection with Ananda, some no spiritual orientation of any kind. They simply liked being there. It certainly was a nice place to live — probably too nice. Our continual challenge was to keep the Community vibration that of an *Ananda* "nice place to live."

At the Mandir we focused on energizing Sunday Services, meditations, classes and other forms of outreach and service. The Living Wisdom School was located both within and adjacent to the Mandir, and brought in a very nice energy. Bent and I also worked a lot with the Portland Ananda ministers — Usha Dermond, Hanuman and Mari Baughman, and Balarama and Sitabai Betts. Both the Betts and the Baughmans served at separate times as community managers during our time in Portland. The role of manager was important but not easy; managers were responsible for maintaining the physical grounds and apartments as well as serving as ministers. We were blessed to work with these two couples; both understood the role and served in the best way possible. We also were blessed to support the development of the Ananda Living Wisdom School (begun by Hanuman and Mari), and to work closely with the main teachers, Usha, and Karen Busch.

During our time in Portland, we went through the Y2K scare and the disaster of 9/11. In response to 9/11, we printed literature and placed it on the front door of the Beaverton Mandir — one way of reaching out to people passing by on the busy street, providing meaning and support in the apocalyptic times we all were experiencing.

Twice while we were there, Swami visited Ananda Portland and gave wonderfully inspiring programs. Even though the talks were well promoted, they were not very well attended. After one of his talks at the Mandir, Swami commented to me, "I meditated as usual before my talk to feel what the people here wanted. What I felt was that they didn't want anything. It wasn't a negative feeling, just a lack of interest." That was our experience too: Many people were happy to come to things, but were less interested in drawing from us spiritually and in activating their own spiritual lives.

Ananda's Presence at the SRF Convocation, Los Angeles (August 2001)

To bring awareness about the SRF lawsuit to their members, a number of us were at the SRF Convocation in 2001, held in downtown Los Angeles. Here is what I wrote about it:

Sunday, August 19, 2001:
Bent and I have just arrived in Los Angeles and are staying at Hotel Stillwell. We are here at the SRF Convocation to pass out literature about the SRF lawsuit against Ananda (now eleven years old!). At the nearby Biltmore Hotel, we've rented a room for Ananda where we can talk with anyone who may have questions about the SRF lawsuit, and about Ananda. David Praver and Asha are in charge of the overall energy; they have done a very nice job prepping Ananda devotees on our purpose in being here and on how to act. Seventy to one hundred Ananda members from our communities and the Village are expected to be here this week. We'll see how it goes!

Signs that we hold up for people to read as we chant:

Why has SRF spent millions of dollars on lawsuits against fellow devotees?

When I am gone, only love can take my place. Where is the love?

August 22, 2001, Wednesday
We leave today from the Burbank airport to return to Portland. After three days (Sunday, Monday, and Tuesday) of chanting Master's chants and showing signs inviting SRF devotees to come to our room at the Biltmore Hotel and view a video of Master and a copy of the original AY, yesterday we held up signs stating specifically why we are here at the Convocation — to persuade SRF to drop the lawsuit against Ananda. SRF members, seeing our signs as they boarded buses for Mother Center and the other shrines

seemed somewhat perplexed and stunned. One man commented to us, "We would never do something like that to you." We called out to him that the lawsuit was in fact happening right now, as we were speaking. Incredible, that after eleven years, this person knows nothing about the lawsuit!

Monday and Tuesday, as we chanted Master's chants to people on their way to various Convocation events, Ananda devotees maintained a sweet, calm, and strong vibration.

Our energy was light-hearted but focused. When Hriman and Padma, and Bent and I, after a morning of chanting and holding up signs, walked into the hotel to have lunch together, we simply put our signs down by our table. We were perfectly at ease doing this, but other diners, mostly SRF members, must have been puzzled.

And so ended our Ananda experience of the 2001 Convocation. Did Ananda's presence there have some energetic influence on the ending of the lawsuit one year later? Who knows? We were simply glad to have tried to bring a greater awareness about this lawsuit to the many SRF members attending the Convocation.

The following year of 2002, the SRF lawsuit, brought against Ananda in 1990, finally ended in Federal court in Sacramento. Ananda was left with $12 million in debt, but also with a sense of freedom not experienced in many years. Over the next ten years we miraculously managed to pay off this debt through the generosity of our members and donors — bringing closure to this intense time of testing and growth.

Interestingly, it was also during the twelve years of the lawsuit that three of the core Ananda communities were established — in Portland, Seattle, and Sacramento.

Leaving Portland

The end of 2003 brought not only our move from Portland to Ananda Village, but the end of twenty-two years of service in Ananda Centers and Communities — from the fall of 1981 to fall of 2003. It had been a time of adventure and intense activity, of tests and blessings. Inwardly, I now felt a major shift coming in my own energy as well.

All during the twenty-two years, especially in the early days in San Francisco, I had felt great blessings from Master and Swami. When I was serving Ananda away from the Village and away from Swami, I didn't miss being near him; always I felt that Swami and Master were with me and helping me. I felt I was able to serve dynamically because of all that Swami had taught me over the years. In everything I had to do and to learn, I knew the real power was in Swami's and Master's energy flowing through me.

It was in understanding that I was acting as a channel that I felt these blessings come.

We Move Back to Ananda Village — An Experience of the "Perfect Joy of St. Francis" (December 28-30, 2003)

Divine Mother seems always to have 'just one more thing' to teach us in this life — but only, of course, if we're willing to see Her hand behind our experiences.

There is a wonderful story from the life of St. Francis — how to recognize perfect joy.

As St. Francis and his close companion, Brother Leo, were walking along on a snowy day, Francis called out to Brother Leo, "Do you know what perfect joy is, Brother Leo?"

Francis goes on to speak of what perfect joy is not — that perfect joy is not found when you *think* you have it, nor when things are going the way you wish them to.

Perfect joy comes when you arrive at the monastery and are not welcomed, are instead reviled, and even beaten by your own brothers. If even then you maintain a feeling of God's joy within you, then you may be assured that you have found the state of perfect joy.

My husband Bent and I were given our own unique opportunity to experience perfect joy.

We had been preparing for our move from the Ananda Portland Community to Ananda Village for some months. We would pack up our apartment, deliver all our boxes to storage at Ananda Village, and then return briefly to Portland to finish up our duties there. In the busyness of our last week of packing, sorting, and cleaning, we'd lost sight of weather patterns between Portland and Ananda Village.

Because we had, several times before, made the same trip in the month of December without problems, we assumed this, our final move, would also be trouble-free.

Freed from our usual ministerial duties in Portland, on Sunday, December 28, at 8:30 am, we set out down the Willamette Valley, hoping to make good time on Interstate 5.

At the end of the valley are Southern Oregon's mountain passes followed by the whole Siskiyou range beyond Mt. Ashland in northern California, then Mt. Shasta and on down into Redding. We thought that if we could just get over the Siskiyou Pass (4,310 feet), we would be home free on into Redding.

We first became aware of what we were up against as we struggled through driving rain down the entire Willamette Valley. It was difficult even to *see* the highway. I began to pray in earnest. I could feel that we were in for quite a day! The more intensely I prayed that Master's blessings be with us that day, the greater the inner joy I felt. Playing recordings of Swami's music and talks, singing along, and praying, my joy began to increase. Both our car and the 24-foot rental truck seemed enclosed in a bubble of grace and joy, protected from harm.

But the intense rains were only the beginning.

We reached Ashland at 1:30 pm. We had stopped only twice, once to refuel the car and once to refuel the truck. Thank God we did! Bent and I both had the same inner feeling: "Don't stop; just keep on driving."

Fortunately, because we had packed food and water in each vehicle, we didn't need to stop for a meal. As we ascended Mt.

Ashland, the snow began to fall, but lightly enough at first that we were able to go, slowly and surely and without chains, up and over the 4,300-foot pass. The time was 2:00 pm. We later learned that by 7:30 pm, Interstate 5 was closed in both directions and remained so for the next 36 to 48 hours!

The snow continued falling on and on as we made our way past Yreka, Weed, and Mt. Shasta. Now I thought our troubles would surely end. But not yet!

The storm had been following us all day; now it was right behind us as we drove on toward the town of Redding. The highway between Mt. Shasta and Redding is steep and winding—many sharp curves and large trucks. Descending the mountain, although it was intense driving, I felt prayer and grace were with us.

4:00 pm: We arrived safely in Redding. We booked into a motel, parked our large rental truck, and felt, at this much lower elevation, relieved and happy to be safely away from snow and mountains. Or so we thought.

After showering and resting for about an hour, we looked out the window of our room to find that several inches of snow had fallen. Just when we thought we had escaped the storm, we found it had followed us all the way to Redding! Rather than trying to drive, we carefully walked across the street to have dinner; as we ate, we watched more and more snow continue to fall and accumulate. Eight more inches fell in Redding by the next morning! A rare occurrence in this Northern California town on the valley floor.

By 9:00 am snow had begun falling again. Could we safely drive out onto the highway? When there was a break in the snowfall, we decided to go for it. We dug our car out, backed both truck and car out of the motel parking lot, and drove very carefully into the gas station below. The moment of truth came as we drove up a small incline to exit the gas station onto the road. The car made it! I kept moving steadily along until I was able to enter the main highway—hoping Bent was behind me. Soon he sped by, and we were off on our second day's driving adventure—and an adventure it was!

When, just a few miles south of Redding, we finally drove out of the snow, it was only to drive into a driving rain and windstorm that felt like a mild hurricane!—so intense that at times I could barely see our truck right in front of me! The radio weather was now broadcasting a strong wind advisory for big trucks, and for the areas we had to drive through. As strong as the wind was as we travelled south, it became even more intense when we turned east, toward Ananda Village. Now I began praying that no strong gust of wind would tip our truck over. By the grace of God, though it did wobble alarmingly, it remained upright and continued moving forward.

We reached Ananda Village at 2:00 pm, in a hard, cold rain, driven by gusts of wind, the water blowing into our storage space. With help from friends, we unloaded the rental truck as carefully and quickly as we could. We were very relieved as we looked forward to a nice hot shower and an evening to relax before driving the car back to Ananda Portland the following day.

But such was not our lot, on this trip to end all trips!

The guest room was warm and cozy, but Divine mother wasn't through testing us yet—our bathwater was lukewarm, and we could find no toilet paper!

Everything seemed to be conspiring to make this trip as difficult as possible.

The next morning, we left early to drop off the rental truck and be on our way—only to find that the drop-off address we'd been given no longer accepted trucks. Once we'd located the new drop-off site, we made good progress much of the way north.

Close to the end of the 600-mile drive, just when we thought we were free and clear, more challenges sprang up. Approaching Portland, we found highway construction backing traffic up for about sixteen miles—an hour of creeping through heavy traffic at a snail's pace.

Then a heavy rain began to fall, and quickly turned to *snow*. As the snowfall grew thicker, traffic remained slow but steady at about 40 mph. My prayer was that no one slide or stop suddenly. Once again, I felt we were enveloped in a bubble of God's grace, protected and uplifted. "Hold a steady course"—like a mantra this phrase kept going through my mind. "Be calm and centered and all will be well." Though uneasy at having no chains or traction tires, we managed to continue on safely.

Our final test came in the last half mile before the entrance to the Ananda Portland Community. The road was snow covered and blocked with flares; we couldn't proceed. Only five minutes before it had been blocked off by the fire department—eight cars were off the road!

Very carefully we managed to turn around, make a big loop on several well-traveled streets, and finally make it into the community and into our apartment. It was 9:45 pm. We had traveled a total of 1200 miles through every imaginable type of intense weather and road conditions without having a breakdown or a major accident. The past two days felt like a miracle of God—a miracle possible because we had remained calm and in tune with God's grace.

"Perfect joy" came to us, I believe, because no matter what came our way, we held ourselves open to it—and to living in a flow of grace, and a bubble of protection.

[LEFT] 1982, San Francisco House

[BELOW] 1982, San Francisco House, street view

1982, San Francisco House, Christmas

1982, Parvati and Dianna

[LEFT] 1983, San Francisco House – Ram and Parvati

[BELOW] 1982, First Yoga Teacher Training course in San Francisco

[LEFT] 1985, Capri, May, Guido Odierna, painting for Kirtani

[BELOW] 1985 Capri, May, with Swami

[ABOVE] 1985, Italy, Parvati and Devi

[LEFT] 1985, Sept, on the train to Capri and Sorrento

[ABOVE] 1985, Villa Rombolotti, May, Swami's birthday

[BELOW] 1985, Villa Rombolotti, May, a staff meeting on the terrazza

1985, Villa Rombolotti, June, Jyotish and Devi departing for America

1985, Villa Rombolotti, September, time for mail

1985, Friends in the US, Anandi, Catherine, Bent, Bharat

1986, Wedding, Swami, Bent, Parvati, Rosanna

1986, Wedding, fire ceremony

1986, Wedding, at the altar

1989, Ananda Assisi Staff: [STANDING] Drupada, Deborah, Helmut, Daniel, Michael, Parvati, Bent; [FRONT] Dianna, Shivani, Mary

[LEFT] 1989, Ananda Assisi, Bent and Parvati, after Sunday Service

[BELOW] 1989, Ananda Assisi, Bent and Parvati, at Il Ritiro

1989, Singing in the Assisi piazza

1988, Sharing Nature
Pilgrimage, Zion Park.
Bharat, Anandi, Parvati

1991, Court case,
Parvati

1991, The Expanding
Light. Parvati on staff,
Bent directing the EL

1994, Texas, Parvati and Bent   1992, Texas, Parvati and Bent, Christmas

[ABOVE] 1994, Dallas, Texas. Our house, Bent, Jan, Parvati, JT Heater

[ABOVE, LEFT] 1994, Texas, Vidura, J.T., Liladevi, Jan, Durga, Parvati, Bent, Eric

[LEFT] 1994, Texas, Jinnae and Roderick, Jan and Robert, Parvati and Bent, Durga and Vidura

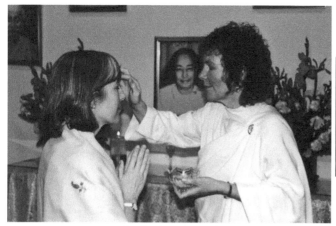

1995, Portland, Parvati and Bent

1995, Portland, Parvati and Paula

1998, Portland, [BACK] Saranya Michael, David, Larkin, Kent, Carianne; [FRONT] Mindy, Karin, Usha, Parvati, Bent, Marilyn

2001, Portland, Parvati, Devi, Jyotish, Bent

[RIGHT] 2001, Portland, Columbia River Gorge. Bharat, Parvati, Anandi

[BELOW] 2001, Portland, Sunday Service, Bent and Parvati, Anandi and Bharat

[BELOW] 2001, Portland, Chinese Garden with Swami. [FROM LEFT] Bent, Dave, Hanuman, Parvati, Swami, Mari, Usha

2001, Portland, a book signing for Swami

2001, Seattle airport, Parvati, Swami, Hriman and Padma

2003, Portland, La Tourelle Falls, Parvati, Jamuna, Bent

1999, Italy, May,
Colony Leader's retreat
with Swami, in Ananda
Assisi

1999, Italy, May,
Colony leader's retreat.
[FROM LEFT] Kirtani,
Vidura, Bent, Maria,
Ananta, Parvati, Padma
and Hriman

1999, Italy, May,
Colony leaders retreat.
Basilica of St. Francis,
the rooms of St. Joseph
of Copertino: [FROM
LEFT] Padma, Dianna,
Maria, Kirtani, a
padre, Jyotish, Shivani,
Ananta, Devi, Ram,
David P, Parvati, David
Hoogandyk, Vidura

Chapter 5

Life at Ananda 2004 to the Present

In waking, eating, working, dreaming, sleeping,
Serving, meditating, chanting, divinely loving,
My soul will constantly hum, unheard by any:
God! God! God!

A Pilgrimage to India!

As previously mentioned, the end of 2003 was also the end of our time serving at Ananda Portland. And it brought an unexpected blessing: a pilgrimage to India! This came from members of Ananda Portland congregation as a way of showing their appreciation for our six years of service there. We were amazed and felt very blessed by their generosity and kindness. This pilgrimage would be our first trip to India. So abundant were the donations from Ananda Portland members in support of this gift that we were able to bring back many gifts for these, our gurubhais and friends during the past six years.

On the pilgrimage, we traveled with a wonderfully international Ananda Assisi pilgrimage group led by Arjuna and Shivani, and Jayadev and Sahaja—Italian, German, English and American devotees.

We visited not only Master's shrines but also Swami Kriyananda at his home in the newly forming Ananda Center in Gurgaon, just outside Delhi.

The pilgrimage sites we visited in India were for the most part associated with the life of Paramhansa Yogananda and our line of gurus: Sri Yukteswar's seaside ashram in Puri; Yogananda's family home and the nearby Tulsi Bose home in Kolkata; Sri Yukteswar's ashram in Serampur (Sri Ram Pur); the Kali temple associated with Master and Sri Ramakrishna in Dakineshwar; the home of Lahiri Mahasaya in Varanasi (Benares). The pilgrimage then traveled north to Rishikesh and Vashishta Guha. It was three and a half weeks long, which allowed us enough time to get a feel for present-day India.

And so, on this high note of inspiration, our time of service in Portland came to a close and we made our final trip to Ananda Village.

Caring for My Mother

A second significant part of the transition from Portland to Ananda Village began in fall of 2002 and continued into spring of 2004: My mother, who had developed lung cancer in 2002, had to be moved to Portland from Ohio (and in 2004, on to Ananda Village) so that I could care for her. For a number of months, the time with my mother was divided between visits to doctors and afternoon coffee outings at the local mall. As intense as these days were for both of us, they did allow us to spend a great deal of quality time together. When I wasn't caring for my mother, I was serving as a spiritual director (together with Bent) for Ananda Portland. My mother's passing in April 2004, coincided with the beginning of a new phase of my life and service at Ananda.

The Janaka Foundation — Estate Planning to Support the Future of Ananda

On March 1, 2004, I began serving as Executive Director of The Janaka Foundation — a radical departure from anything I had experienced in my entire life with Ananda. Though there had long been the need for estate planning as a means of securing the future of Ananda, we weren't able to take definite steps in this direction until 2004.

Looking back, I am amazed at the precise timing of my first days with The Janaka Foundation: March 1, 2004, I began work with Janaka; April 26, 2004, my mother passed away; a week later, the beginning of May, I was on my way to a Planned Giving seminar in Chicago.

My mother's death provided me with a hands-on introduction to estate planning. Because she had done a very good job with her own planning, and because I was now the beneficiary of her efforts, I understood from my own direct experience the importance of doing estate planning, and doing it well. If done thoughtfully, such planning can help your family and friends, and the causes that are important to you, during the difficult time that can come after the death of someone close to you.

Indiana University offered a three-day course on the Fundamentals of Planned Giving, a course considered one of their most difficult. Whatever my misgivings, I took the plunge. I remember thinking at the time, "Really, does this program have to be in *Chicago?*" But when I arrived, I was greatly encouraged to find myself in a room full of people like me — people who worked for good causes and organizations that wanted to help people, but who knew nothing about estate planning. Being in the city itself was not a concern; we had very little time to see any of it! After each intense workshop, I would leave the hotel and walk quickly down the street to Chicago's Miracle Mile — my way to absorb energetically the information being presented.

By the following year, 2005, I understood the need to establish an actual planned giving program. Periodic mailings wouldn't be enough. Just when I finally understood the need for a professional consultant, and found one to hire, The Janaka Foundation ran out of money! At this crucial moment in time, I felt Divine Mother and Master showing me they did want Ananda to have this program happen: One of my gurubhais passed away, leaving her estate to Janaka — not a huge amount of money, but enough for us to continue moving forward.

Following the helpful guidance of the consultant I had hired, I began sending out quarterly newsletters and speaking directly to people I knew would be interested in estate planning. The phrase "Include Ananda in Your Will" I put on my mailings and asked other Ananda departments to do so also. Realizing that people didn't usually think of supporting Ananda in this way, I wanted to make it clear that we *welcomed* planned gifts from an estate, and to show people in the quarterly newsletters how to go about doing this kind of planning. To let our donors know how much we appreciated their estate planning gifts, I not only thanked them directly, but also established the Janaka Legacy Fellowship as a way of recognizing their thoughtful planning.

During my first twelve years with Janaka (2004–2015), my steady focus was on promoting estate planning that included Ananda. Little by little, the idea took hold. Having established Ananda's ability and readiness to receive estate gifts, along with how they can be made, we then focused on showing our donors how we would use their gifts. During these first twelve years we received a modest flow of estate gifts. For these I am eternally grateful! Then in 2016, The Janaka Foundation received an estate gift of $2.23 million from a long-time donor and member of Ananda. This very generous estate gift was a game-changer for us. We were then able to establish a $1.1 million Ananda Endowment Fund as well as a Future Grants Fund. In addition, and as a way to celebrate, we gave generously to core areas of Ananda worldwide. Establishing both the Endowment and Future Grants funds finally gave us a way to demonstrate to donors how their estate gifts would be used.

Since 2016, the Ananda Janaka Foundation (as we have now named it) has become a magnet for drawing estate gifts to Ananda. Our Annual Report shows how these gifts are supporting Ananda's mission through Grants, with the final page showing photos of the board of directors — the long-time members of Ananda responsible for directing estate gifts to various areas of our work.

The increasing generosity of our donors shows how important estate gifts are to the future of Ananda.

Swami's Final Decade of Service (2003–2013)

Ananda in India

The last years of Swami's life were a whirlwind of activity! In the fall of 2003, as Bent and I were finishing up our time in Ananda Portland, we heard that an American couple living in India had connected with Swami about Yogananda's work there. Their conversation brought to Swami the realization that here was the moment he had been waiting for — the time to bring an Ananda presence to India. By November of that year, he and the group of Ananda members he asked to join him had moved into a mansion in Gurgaon.

Before this move, Swami had been inspired to write a second book based on the notes from his time with Master. The first, *The Essence of Self-Realization*, had been organized to show Master's comments on Self-realization. The second book, *Conversations with Yogananda*, printed in India in 2003 and organized simply by number, Swami used as a way to introduce Indians to Yogananda, and to launch Ananda's work there. By fall of 2004, he was recording videos, ten or more each day, based on the *Conversations* book. The videos appeared on one of India's most popular spiritual television channels. For us at Ananda, Swami's dynamic first steps in India were a thrilling time.

During our Pilgrimage trip to India in 2004, we had a one-and-a-half hour satsang with Swami Kriyananda at the newly established Ananda ashram in Gurgaon. Because our time with Swami was so limited (the pilgrimage group was moving on to Rishikesh), I returned again that fall with Seva for a two-week visit. While we were there, Swami asked Seva to stay on in India and serve there, leaving me to travel back from India by myself. Then came one of the most interesting coincidences I've experienced. As I was having something to eat in the Minneapolis airport, someone called my name: "Parvati." My immediate thought was, "But I don't know anyone here." And then I looked up, and there was

Bent! I had known he'd be traveling to visit family in Canada, but not the exact route. We discovered that his entry gate was next to mine, just down the hallway. This provided a fun time to share a little about my visit with Swami. I couldn't help feeling that Divine Mother had arranged for our paths to cross, briefly and unexpectedly, in this Minneapolis airport!

The Essence of the Bhagavad Gita: "Give Me Thy Heart!"

In the fall of 2005, Bent and I again made plans to visit Swami and Ananda's newly developing work in India. We arrived at a momentous time—Swami was just finishing the writing of *The Essence of the Bhagavad Gita*. Staying in Gurgaon at the Ananda ashram house, each morning we walked to Swami's house nearby, then spent several hours reading the amazing commentaries he was writing on the Gita.

It was a thrilling time!

Now, in mid-November, Swami had been writing continuously since early October. The manuscript pages were printed out and now piled high on the coffee table in his living room. From time to time, Swami would slowly walk down the marble steps from his third-floor office to add what he had just finished writing. One morning toward the end of our visit, he came down the stairs saying, "I've just gotten to the part where Krishna says, 'Give Me thy heart!'" What was flowing through him was clearly keeping Swami in an uplifted blissful state. It felt as though Master and Swami were living in the house together, working to bring this new scripture into manifestation. It was a deeply blessed time to be with Swami.

It was also during this intense period of writing that Swami gave Bent a spiritual name. Bent had requested this before we arrived in India. For this special occasion, Swami invited the two of us up to his sitting room. Then Swami gave him the name Pranaba—

a name which, he explained, meant the "cosmic sound of AUM" and was to be spelled with a 'b' not a 'v' as is sometimes done in India. This day also happened to be Pranaba's birthday, now doubly blessed by Swami's gift of a spiritual name and a mala. Later that day a small group of us went for coffee at the nearby Metro Mall—for Swami a break from writing, for us a time to celebrate with him. The entire time of our visit came just as Swami was finishing the writing of this great scripture— *The Essence of the Bhagavad Gita*.

In early December, to celebrate finishing his writing, Swami invited a group of us to dine with him at a beautiful hotel nearby. A few days after this, Pranaba and I departed India, and flew home to California and Ananda Village. We felt deeply blessed by all that we had experienced during our time with Swami—especially in having a direct experience of the energy and consciousness that made *The Essence of the Bhagavad Gita* possible.

A Succession of Major New Books

Back at Ananda Village, we arrived just in time to help prepare for the book launch of the Gita, now planned for June of 2006. The launch itself would be at the Herbst Theater in downtown San Francisco, with a beautiful fundraising dinner at the Palace Hotel the night before. The launch met with wonderful success and was the first of a number of book launches during the last years of Swami's life—each one a book he felt inspired to write to continue his work for Master.

By the next year, 2007, Swami had completed the *Revelations of Christ* book, subsequently launched at the Wadsworth Theater in Los Angeles. The night before the event, we stayed at the Intercontinental Hotel to help with a fundraising dinner in their banquet room. It was from this book launch that Ananda's work in the Los Angeles area began.

Over the next six years, and until his death in April 2013, Swami continued to be active in completing the numerous projects he felt Master wanted him to do.

Books published during these years included:

2008 — *In Divine Friendship*

2009 — *The New Path* (introduced by an event at the outdoor Ford theater in Los Angeles)

2011 — *Paramhansa Yogananda: A Biography* (also at the Ford Theater)

2012 — *The Time Tunnel* and *Demystifying Patanjali* (with a fundraising tea in Los Angeles, and a final event at the Ford Theater)

2013 — *A Pilgrimage to Guadalupe: The Soul's Final Journey*

Pranaba and I attended the events held at the Ford Theater. We would drive from the Village to Los Angeles, sometimes spending the night halfway there. We would then spend a few nights in the L.A. area, attend the events, and drive back to the Village at the end of the weekend. These years were intense — filled with spiritual blessings flowing out from Swami as he approached the end of this magnificent incarnation.

The Nayaswami Order (2009)

In 2009, Swamiji established a new expression of India's ancient Swami Order, one especially geared to renunciates in our times: the Nayaswami Order. He moved forward quickly with a small book explaining the principles underlying the order, the need for the new expression to fit the new age, vows for different levels of commitment and the colors associated with each vow. Though I imagine Swami had been contemplating such an order for some time, the actual expression in writing and ceremony all took place quite quickly while he was living at Ananda Assisi. The rapid emergence of the new order felt like a natural evolution in Ananda's world mission.

For many at Ananda, no matter what outward position they might hold, the ideal of renunciation was always deeply there. By establishing the Renunciate order, Swami was giving us the gift of a way to reaffirm our own deep inner commitment to God and Guru; to join him in a level of renunciation that he had committed himself to throughout his own lifetime.

He called together a group of Ananda members, those living in Assisi as well as in Ananda in America and India, to take the vow from him. The gathering was not large in numbers but was strong in those who had dedicated their lives to God and Guru. Swami had long envisioned the order in a very broad way—as an order for those of any organization or spiritual path who felt in tune with the ideals it represented. In this respect, it was similar to the Swami Order of India, established by the Adi Shankara in the eighth century CE.

This first initiation took place in November 2009 in Ananda Assisi's Temple of Light. A second initiation with Jyotish and Devi took place the following month at Ananda Village on December 24, 2009. Learning that Swami had requested those wishing to take the Nayaswami vow ask his permission, Pranaba and I each emailed him and soon received his approval. As I read over the vow, the thought came into my mind, "This is my vow. This is how I feel about my life and about my spiritual goals." It did not feel like an overwhelming commitment—rather it felt familiar, like a direction I had been going in my entire spiritual life. This is not to say that I felt I had perfected the vow in my own life, but more that it represented my natural spiritual commitment, and had always been there.

For the ceremony at the Village a fire was placed at the center of the room. All at one time those taking the vow did "danda pranam"—lying face-down on the floor, offering themselves completely to God.

The following is the vow we took:

The Vow of Complete Renunciation

From now on,
I embrace as the only purpose of my life
the search for God.

I will never take a partner,
or, if I am married, I will look upon my partner
as belonging only to Thee, Lord.
In any case, I am complete in myself,
and in myself will merge all the opposites of duality.

I no longer exist as a separate entity,
but offer my life unreservedly
into Thy great Ocean of Awareness.

I accept nothing as mine, no one as mine,
no talent, no success, no achievement as my own,
but everything as Thine alone.

I will feel that not only the fruit of my labor,
but the labor itself, is only Thine.
Act through me always, Lord,
to accomplish Thy design.

I am free in Thy joy,
and will rejoice forever
in Thy blissful presence.

Help me in my efforts
to achieve perfection in this, my holy vow.
For I have no goal in life
but to know Thee,
and to serve as Thy channel of blessing
to all mankind.

The day of initiation was filled with the blessings of Master and Swami as we dedicated our lives once again, joyfully and gratefully, and ever more completely, to the ongoing search for God.

A Los Angeles Ashram (2010)

In 2010, Swami felt inspired to move to Los Angeles and spent the better part of the next year sharing Master with all who came to the satsangs he offered — on Master's teachings and mission, and on the consciousness of Master as Swami had known him. Jyotish and Devi came to help with Swami's work; and, as an expression of Ananda's presence, a Los Angeles ashram house came into being.

A Final Personal Blessing from Swami

On May 11, 2011, Swami invited Pranaba and me to his apartment at Crystal Hermitage. There he personally blessed Pranaba as a Kriyacharya. After the blessing, gazing at the two of us standing before him, he said to us, "Bless you in all that you do." To us Swami seemed in a deeply blissful state.

June of 2012 was the last time I had a personal contact with Swami — brief, simple and sweet, at a fundraising tea at Bharavi's home in West Los Angeles; the tea was followed by an event that evening at the Ford Theater. In September, Swami returned to the Bay area for a final satsang at a local college — a satsang that turned out to be the last time most of us would be with him in person.

Demystifying Patanjali (Summer 2012)

That summer Swami also wrote *Demystifying Patanjali*, a clear, accessible commentary on a great saint whose yoga sutras had too often been explained in an overly erudite and scholarly way. It had been on his mind to write this book for some time. That August, while he was writing it, Pranaba and I once again began teaching a week-long course on the Yoga Sutras at The Expanding Light.

Though we had taught the course several times since 2008, now, since Swami himself was deeply immersed in Patanjali's teachings, he was available to us for questions about several subtle points. Through Swami's guidance we were able to understand the sutras on a deeper level. It was a very special time for us to be teaching this course.

Before he left the U.S. that fall, Swami wrote *The Time Tunnel*, a book about time travel—for children of all ages. In fact, the entire summer of 2012 was full of activity! Filming the *Finding Happiness* movie dominated the energy at the Village for a number of weeks, taking over specific areas of the Village in turn: the downtown area and Master's Market; The Expanding Light; Crystal Hermitage; and some of the residents' homes.

At the beginning of 2013, the completed *Finding Happiness* movie was brought to Swami in Gurgaon, India. We heard how much the film pleased him, and his reaction to the Ananda residents' participation—words to the effect, "You all are so naturally yourselves!"

Passings: "We Will Always Be Friends"

That summer was also a time when several close, and long-time members came to the end of their lives. Even as scenes from *Finding Happiness* were being filmed nearby at Crystal Hermitage, Nayaswami Lila, Swami's cook and helper, passed away. I was blessed to help with her care in her last days, and to be present when Swami came to visit her. It was a brief final meeting. Swami, unsteady and having trouble walking, spoke to Lila about the projects he was working on, as he had always done over the seventeen years she had served him. He then looked at her and said, "We will always be friends." Lila, who was still able to sit up in bed, looked at Swami and responded, "We will always be friends." Before he left Swami repeated, "We will always be friends." Two days later Lila passed peacefully in her room at Crystal Hermitage.

Tim Kretzmann, another long-time member of Ananda, also came to the end of his life within days of Lila's passing. For two consecutive nights, large Astral Ascension ceremonies were held in the Yogananda Amphitheater at Lotus Lake. The amphitheater was filled with Village residents and friends, gathered to say a sad, but also joyous, farewell to these dear friends and gurubhais with whom we had spent so many years on the spiritual path.

Swami Kriyananda's Passing

THE NIGHT OF SWAMI'S PASSING (APRIL 21, 2013)

On April 21, 2013, about eight in the morning, Swami Kriyananda passed away at his home in Ananda Assisi. We had felt for some years that he would soon be leaving his body. When the moment of transition came, he went very quickly. After fifteen minutes of trouble breathing and a small seizure, he was gone.

That morning Swami had followed his usual routine, rising early, going to his desk, checking emails — his way of keeping in touch with the far-flung Ananda spiritual family. Then came a twenty-second seizure. Just before this, Miriam, his nurse, had asked him if he would agree to certain routine medical tests; she was concerned because he seemed particularly withdrawn that morning. His last word to her questioning was, "Anything." Then came the seizure and the difficulty breathing. Miriam and others took Swami in and laid him on his bed, hoping to find a position to enable him to breathe more easily. Very shortly, with a few last breaths, he was gone.

At that same time, at 11:40 pm California time, we at the Village received a call from Dr. Peter letting us know that Swami had passed. Our phone had rung a few minutes before that, but I was sound asleep and only heard the ringing as in a dream. I woke up too late to catch it; when I checked, the message simply said Swami was having trouble breathing. A few minutes later the phone rang again, this time with Dr. Peter saying he was gone.

I didn't often email Swami, but I had done so earlier that same evening. I wasn't sure whether to send the email, but clicked the

send button around 10:00 pm our time that night. I didn't expect
a reply, but just wanted Swami to know that I had been thinking of
him that day as I hosted people coming to Springtime at Ananda.

Here is what I sent him:

-----Original Message-----

From: Parvati Hansen

Sent: Saturday, April 20, 2013, 9:56 PM

To: Swami

Subject: Springtime at Ananda!

Dear Swamiji,

It was an astral day today at the Crystal Hermitage
gardens. All the flowers were simply glowing, with
incredibly beautiful colors and arrangements of
colors. And people visiting were so very happy
to be there.

I felt your presence the entire morning as I stood
at the bottom of the stairs by the front door of
the Hermitage greeting the hundreds of people
that came today. They were simply awestruck by
the beauty they found in the gardens. When I
left a little after 1pm, close to 500 people had
already come through.

One man was of particular interest. He was one
of the people who had come from Yogi Bhajan's
group to help us rebuild the community after the
fire in 1976. This man was simply amazed by what
we had been able to accomplish since that time.
He thanked me several times for what we have
created, both at the Hermitage and with Ananda as
a whole. He said that even in 1976 the group who

came to help us rebuild had felt blessed by being
at Ananda and the people they met then.

In Master's love,

Parvati

Later I was curious to know if Swami had opened my email, so
I asked Lakshman, Swami's secretary, if he would check:
On April 21, 2013 — from Lakshman:

"I just checked, and he did -- the next-to-last
message that he read. :-)"

Because we've all worked together for so many years, and have
long-standing friendships, the needed arrangements following
Swami's passing came together in a smooth flow.

Pranaba and I stayed up that evening to call people here at the
Village, and then Center leaders and friends farther afield. Later we
heard how much people appreciated receiving those calls.

Jyotish and Devi, after talking with Anand and Kirtani, made
reservations to fly to Italy that Sunday evening. Pranaba and I
stayed behind. My thought was that we should be available to be
with people in the Village. A few Village residents felt they should
be in Assisi; most of the colony leaders from the US and India flew
there as well.

My feelings were a natural mixture of great joy for Swami and
for his freedom in God, and sadness that such an incredible lifetime with him had come to a close. One word that came often to
mind in this time was "seamless," — a seamless flow of events after
his passing and in how I myself felt. Swami is everywhere, and
in everything at Ananda Village. All of Ananda has grown out of
his inspiration. For forty-five years he has infused us with Master's
consciousness; now he has given us the opportunity to carry on in
the same spirit.

Almost two months later, the time of transition had come to feel familiar—that is, that we, as a spiritual family, have in other lives been through a time of Swami leaving us and our carrying on with the work after his passing. We know what to do; we're now moving on into the future with this work. Swami and Master have given us the blessed opportunity to dedicate the rest of our lives to carrying on their great mission—now our great adventure.

Later in 2013, filming for *The Answer* movie began at Ananda Village. Although the film wasn't completed until the following year, the making of the film felt like a completion of part of Swami's life and mission.

A Dream about Swami Kriyananda

Mike Wolverton, a gurubhai and friend from Dallas, Texas, later shared with me a dream he experienced after visiting The Expanding Light the weekend Swami passed.

"I'm Going Over Now!"

[A DREAM I HAD ABOUT SWAMIJI ON THE NIGHT HE PASSED AWAY]

"For twenty years I had been a core member of the Ananda Dallas Center. I was visiting Ananda Village in April 2013. I left the Village on Saturday, April 20 to visit my sister in Sacramento, where we planned to spend a couple of nights at a local hotel before I flew back to Texas.

"I went to bed at 9:00 pm, and awoke at 3:30 am, Sunday, April 21. Upon awakening, I realized I had just had an amazing dream, my first one with Swamiji in it.

"In the dream, Swamiji and I were holding a large pole. It was light in weight but had a diameter of around 10 inches. Swamiji and I were each holding one end of the pole, which was very long. I realized that the idea was that Swamiji was going to pole vault using the pole.

"We then both began running, and at one point I planted my end in the ground. Swamiji was going up on the other end and it was taking him very high. I wasn't sure if he would make this very high pole-vault, and I thought, 'The audacity of him trying to make it!' So, I began trying to help him by pushing on the pole from where I was standing.

"At that point, Swamiji, who was by now very high up, called out clearly, 'I'm going over now!'

"With that, the dream ended. I learned later that day that Swamiji had left his body that same morning at his home in Assisi.

"I realized before the news of his passing that Swamiji was communicating his liberation to me, as well as his encouragement, to try to live ever more profoundly in the Divine Reality. I felt that he was giving me the honor of trying to help him, and the Ananda movement, by 'pushing on the pole.'"

A Milestone Since Swami's Passing

Here is what I wrote on *June 13, 2013*:

"I thought to write about Swami's passing as today we passed another milestone. After the morning meditation at the Crystal Hermitage dome, about 8:00 am, we moved the closed casket containing his body out of the dome, where it has been since May 2. The casket was lowered into a temporary burial plot behind his apartment at the Hermitage. Here it will rest until the Swami Kriyananda Moksha Mandir is built and dedicated.

"During the past six weeks his casket has rested in the Crystal Hermitage dome; each morning community residents have gathered to meditate with our dear friend and guide. It has been a sweet time of deep inspiration. Now that this time has ended, we are moving into the next phase of this transition — our life without Swami's physical presence."

"Swami Is Very Much with You Right Now."

Several years after Swami Kriyananda's passing, a swami in Rishikesh, whom many there see as a saint, expressed his high regard for Swami Kriyananda. To several Ananda leaders he said, "Swamiji is very much with you right now." As we moved forward with Ananda's work in the world, I too have felt his energy, joy, and support with me, have felt his presence strongly.

I continued my service, begun in 2004, directing The Janaka Foundation. I felt that the effort I was putting out to encourage people to include Ananda in their estate planning would bear fruit in the years ahead. And so it has done.

Moksha Mandir

It was during 2014 that building began on the final resting place for Swami's body, the Moksha Mandir at Crystal Hermitage.

At the dedication of this beautiful Mandir in the Spring of 2015, hundreds of Ananda members came from around the world; probably the largest gathering to date at Ananda Village. A few days earlier, on Swami's birthday, May 19, 2015, the casket containing his body had been moved to a specially prepared place beneath the floor of the Mandir. Its location is indicated inside the Mandir by engravings in a roped-off area of the floor.

This beautiful and spiritually expansive temple, dedicated to Swami Kriyananda and to his moksha (final liberation), has become a focal point for many who visit Crystal Hermitage. I have noticed that during the Springtime at Ananda event held each year during April and May, among the thousands who come to view the gardens, many also look inside the Mandir, only to end up spending time there meditating or praying, deeply touched by their experience.

Nayaswami Jyotish: Swami's Spiritual Successor, the Ananda Dharmacharya

The years following Swami Kriyananda's passing were filled with a great deal of activity for Ananda.

On Swami's death, Nayaswami Jyotish became the Ananda Dharmacharya, Ananda's spiritual leader. He and his wife, Nayaswami Devi, serve together also as Spiritual Directors for Ananda Worldwide. The still evolving work in India, begun by Swami in 2003, continues under their supportive leadership. Beginning in 2013 and ongoing into the future are Jyotish and Devi's annual visits to Ananda India, as well as to Ananda Assisi in its central role of serving Europe and beyond.

I continued to feel Swami's presence in my life and in my service, especially in my work with the Ananda Janaka Foundation. The large estate gift we received in 2016 was, I felt, a blessing from Swamiji's lifetime of dedication to fulfilling Yogananda's mission in this world—from his unwavering adherence to being a true disciple to his guru. The gift was particularly meaningful coming as it did during the week of the third anniversary of Swami's passing. As I stood at the computer and watched these funds flow into the Ananda Janaka bank account, I thought of the many years Swami had spent bringing Ananda into being. It was a touching moment for me.

A Return Visit to Ananda Assisi

In the fall of 2016, Pranaba and I made a visit to Ananda Assisi. It was the first time we had been there since 1999, when Swami called all the Ananda Community leaders together to discuss Ananda's work. This time we came simply to see how this part of the work had evolved and to connect directly with friends and gurubhais we'd stayed in touch with since living there in 1989–90. It was wonderful to see how the work had expanded and to be with friends we had served with many years before.

Intercontinental Kriyaban Retreat, at Ananda Assisi (August 27–September 4, 2017)

The following year, 2017, we unexpectedly again visited Ananda Assisi, this time to participate in an Intercontinental Kriyaban Retreat. Initially, I wasn't looking forward to another visit so soon, especially to an event that would draw hundreds of people to Ananda Assisi's small retreat campus. My thought was that it would be too crowded to enjoy such an event. But, as you will see, my actual experience was very different from what I had imagined.

The following is my account written soon after our return to America:

"The Intercontinental Kriyaban Retreat was an extraordinary event in Ananda's history—a living demonstration that, four and a half years after Swami Kriyananda's passing, Ananda is growing dynamically, and organically, on three continents—the Americas, Europe, and India, as well as Russia, China, Singapore, and beyond.

"A number of us arrived at the Rome airport on Friday morning, August 25, from both coasts of America, and from several Ananda centers in India. It was wonderful to see and greet one another. We were taken to a lovely nearby hotel, the Golden Tulip, to rest and recover from our long overseas trips with a quick breakfast and a refreshing swim in the hotel pool. It was a wonderful way to enter into Italy and the adventure that awaited us!

"That evening our dinner was served outside, overlooking the pool. A good night's sleep, another very enjoyable hotel breakfast, and then we were on our way to Assisi. Driving through Assisi brought memories of past inspiration from this city of St. Francis, especially of the saint's deep spiritual connection with Master, Swami, and Ananda.

"From the town of Assisi, we drove the sixteen kilometers to the Ananda retreat center. As we approached the center, large, beautiful flags lined the road to welcome visitors. It somehow felt astral to me. The focus for the first weekend program was to bless the new Temple of Joy. Even in its unfinished state, the new temple, and the recently purchased land it occupies, represented a major step forward in the development of Ananda Assisi.

"Jyotish and Devi, who had been giving programs at Ananda Assisi for a number of weeks, led an outdoor fire ceremony and blessing for the temple after Sunday Service. (It was quite a challenge to stand in the sun for the ceremony on this scorching hot day!) In a nearby town, the weekend guests had already attended a showing of *The Answer*, the newly finished film of Swami's life with Master.

"After lunch, the weekend guests gradually departed; those staying on for the Kriyaban Retreat, about two hundred people, including twenty-two kriyacharyas from America, Europe, and India, attended an orientation that evening.

"Kriyabans came from many different countries and spoke many languages—Italian, German, Russian, Croatian, Spanish, English, Hindi. The talks that week were simultaneously translated into a number of languages: It was extraordinary to experience directly not a jumble of languages and cultures, but the underlying unity of consciousness of a culturally diverse group of people who share the powerful common bond born of their daily practice of Kriya Yoga. I thought, 'This is what world brotherhood feels like.' Absorbed in this experience, this retreat was for me the most inspiring Ananda event I've ever attended.

"The weather remained very hot throughout the six days of the Retreat. Windows were kept open at night for air; even at seven in the morning, when we meditated together in a large open-sided tent, the temperature was quite warm—even hot in the direct sunlight.

"Ananda Assisi excels in making their European guests feel welcome; most programs provide simultaneous translations into Italian, German, and English. The Kriyaban Retreat went beyond even these three languages, to accommodate a number of others. Some groups, the Russians among them, brought their own translator. Throughout there was a beautiful flow, the expression of a truly cooperative spirit that met everyone's needs.

"I was also pleasantly surprised to see a number of friends—among them, Jamey and Darlene Potter from Portland. (Their son, Julian, now living at Ananda Assisi, is the architect for the new Temple of Joy.) Narayani and Shurjo were there from Spain; and Gordana and Emil from Croatia who are long-time Ananda members.

"I was touched to hear from a number of people there that they had enjoyed seeing my Sunday Services online — their words brought a more personal dimension to Ananda's online outreach to devotees all over the world.

An Email I Sent to Nayaswami Shivani at Ananda Assisi (September 18, 2017)

Please thank everyone there for their part in the Kriyaban Retreat.

For their content, and especially for their vibration, the classes by the Kriyacharyas were amazing. So little ego was expressed that I felt Master, Swamiji, and Babaji flowing through the speakers. All through the week I felt our masters dynamically present.

Complementing the deep vibration coming through the speakers was the wonderful uplifting presence of the many kriyabans from Europe, America, and India. There was a pervasive happiness that brought everyone together into a united group—a wonderful example of true world brotherhood.

My dominant impression was of Ananda's expansive energy worldwide, a dynamic, joyful expression of Master's mission responding to the enthusiastic openness of seekers everywhere.

A Return Visit to Ananda India

In 2018, Pranaba and I decided it was time to see Ananda's work in India. Our travels to India in 2004 and 2005 had been to see Swamiji. Now we wanted to see the fruit of his labors — how the work in India had grown since his passing.

Landing in Mumbai in early October 2018, we spent the next week at the Ananda center in Pune, located in a pleasant area of the city and with a thriving group of devotees, some living in apartments near the center and some commuting from homes nearby. We took part in center events and led some programs ourselves.

The next three weeks we spent in Delhi, dividing our time between attending and giving programs and seeing the city. Pranaba went on the four-day Babaji's Cave pilgrimage; I stayed behind, nursing an ankle I had twisted only days before the pilgrimage! While Pranaba experienced Babaji's Cave, I experienced the local hospital (no broken bones, just bruising); then, staying with Sangeeta in her apartment near the Pancheel Park Delhi center, I had time to myself and time for my ankle to recover.

At the end of October, we flew back to America from Delhi, very glad to have seen several of the major areas of Ananda's work in India.

The Pavilion of Gratitude (June 16, 2019)

June 16, 2019, just two weeks before the Temple of Light opened, marked the dedication of the Pavilion of Gratitude, the completion of a several years' project. The beautiful small outdoor temple — simple in design, astral in feeling — sits on the far side of Lotus Lake, across from the Yogananda Amphitheater, and in walking distance to the Temple of Light and The Expanding Light retreat center. The Pavilion of Gratitude is a place for meditation and remembrance.

Ananda's 50th Anniversary and Temple of Light Dedication at Ananda Village

(JUNE 30–JULY 7, 2019)

2019 was an amazing year for all of Ananda! From June 30th through July 7th, we celebrated the 50th Anniversary of Ananda's founding and also dedicated the new Temple of Light at Ananda Village during the same week. We invited the worldwide Ananda family to be part of the celebration. The months and years leading up to these events were intensely active — planning the Temple and the 50th anniversary event, raising the funds needed, and keeping the international Ananda family well informed of how things were progressing.

To understand the miraculous coming together of people and energy that resulted in the 50th Anniversary Celebration, we need to look back in time. Through the years, Ananda has been able to accomplish a lot with limited resources and people. One reason this has been possible is our ability to work together cooperatively and harmoniously — and, most importantly, to do so in attunement with the leadership and guidance of Swami Kriyananda and the grace of our gurus. The Temple project was so much greater than we could imagine taking on; only a spirit of discipleship, trust in the guidance of Swami and Master, the very generous support of our donors, and the willingness to give our all-in cooperative effort opened the door to God's grace manifesting as the Temple of Light.

THE TEMPLE OF LIGHT

The Temple of Light was a massive project for us; we ended up raising over $3.8 million.

The detailed planning process began in earnest in 2017. The Temple would include a main sanctuary, a dome, classrooms, shoe rooms, vestry, sound booth, entry way, lighting, A/C, heating, bathrooms, as well as extensive landscaping, walkways, and parking.

The building would serve not only as a Temple of Light for Ananda worldwide, but also as the Temple for Ananda Village. It would be the first building ever built as a temple at the Village in fifty years; for the previous thirty-five years we had used the large classroom at The Expanding Light as a Village temple, as well as for many other functions. The new building would keep its main sanctuary specifically as a temple and have separate classrooms for other purposes.

The Temple site was dedicated in the spring of 2018. At the center point of the planned foundation, Jyotish and Devi placed a metal yantra, a symbol emanating blessings and spiritual power.

After the dedication of the site, the building process for the Temple began in earnest. Not long after the foundation was poured, the exterior of the building began to take shape. Even as Pranaba and I were giving Sunday service that summer in the nearby Yogananda Amphitheater, the massive beams for the dome of the Temple were being lifted into place. Nakula, the construction manager, had warned us that noise that day would be unavoidable. Once the roof frame was in place and covered, a team of specialists came in to install the custom-made blue roofing tiles. We were awestruck as we watched this giant sacred structure take shape before our eyes.

During the final months leading up to the June/July dedication, we all hoped for the best and continued moving forward as quickly as we could. Here especially we experienced the fruits of living our spiritual teachings—a balance of non-attachment and dynamic, willing energy.

In May 2019 we held a Seva Week—an opportunity for the larger Ananda spiritual family to be part of the process, helping with the finishing and cleanup work needed before the final push to complete the building.

When the custom-ordered chairs arrived the week before the event, a number of us went over to unload the truck and store the chairs in one of the classrooms until the carpeting could be installed. With careful stacking, five hundred chairs all fit in one room! That same week, we learned that the carpet for the Sanctuary had made it as far as Nevada only to have its transport truck break down! As a last-minute fix, a local company agreed to install a blue carpet they had in stock to hold us over until the specially ordered, higher quality carpet could arrive—and to split the additional cost with us.

On the temporary carpet we set up the five hundred chairs in a specific pattern to accommodate the guests arriving that Sunday.

One last obstacle: the final inspection of the building on Friday, June 28. Though it is almost unheard of for such a complex building to pass its final inspection on the first filing, the Temple of Light sailed through. The builders were astounded! We saw it as one more in the series of miracles that brought the Temple of Light to legal completion in time for the celebration.

On Sunday, June 30, Anandi and Bharat led our last outdoor Sunday service in the Yogananda Amphitheater. The first use of the new Temple would be for welcoming our guests that evening.

As we watched people streaming into the new Temple of Light that evening, we realized that this celebration was the first time in the history of Ananda that we had been able to accommodate our entire spiritual family from around the world in one place, at one time. As Pranaba and I stood at the back of the Temple sanctuary watching people enter, there was an overwhelming feeling of universal happiness—we were caught up in the charged and joyful energy of our spiritual family entering for the first time the Temple of Light.

It was wonderful to see how easily Panduranga Heater's masterful building design allowed people to naturally tune into the special use areas: shoe rooms with cubbies for shoes with integrated small benches to help people taking shoes off and on; unobtrusively planned bathrooms on either side of the "hall of the masters"; a classroom on each side of the entryway, to accommodate overflows from the Temple sanctuary; a wonderfully large concrete entry area at the front of the building to help keep dirt and mud outside. The building was perfectly adapted to people's needs, and it was also expansive, uplifting, and conducive to meditation. It was perfect.

During the following week we hosted as many as nine hundred people at any one time in the Temple, always with the same feeling of harmonious flow that accompanied the building project. During the long planning process for this event — as we looked at the complex logistics of feeding and housing such numbers, arranging parking and transportation around the Village, organizing a flow to sadhanas, classes, meals, special events that would be inspiring for everyone — we could not have imaged the harmonious, effortless flow that blessed the whole week. A continuous miracle!

50th Anniversary of Ananda and Dedication of the Temple of Light:

Welcoming the Light! A week of celebration

Sunday evening Jyotish and Devi set the tone for the week with "Welcoming the Light" — embracing those attending with loving energy.

The schedule for the week was carefully designed to reflect what guests to The Expanding Light were used to. Care was taken to begin and end events on time, to allow free time between them, and to end the evening programs early enough for a good night's rest.

Monday through Sunday included morning *sadhana* (energization, chanting, meditation) in three locations: Temple of Light, Meditation Retreat, Crystal Hermitage.

Breakfast was served where people were staying (The Expanding Light, Meditation Retreat, and the nearby Shady Creek Retreat).

Morning class in the Temple of Light was preceded by chanting and followed by noon meditation.

To make the programs more affordable and because service was such a good way for people to enter into the spirit of the week, we offered a special rate for those wishing to serve.

For lunch and dinner (catered by a local business), The Expanding Light dining room was set up with four serving lines. Guests were able to move through the lines quickly, then find a place to sit in the landscaped area or in one of the two large outdoor tents — roomy, comfortable structures that allowed friends old and new to make connections with fellow devotees from around the world.

Throughout the day Ananda buses shuttled guests to classes, around the Village, and to and from the camping area at Shady Creek.

The morning classes expressed a high level of consciousness — filled with inspiration and the light of our masters. The Temple's translation booths allowed simultaneous translations into Spanish, Italian, and Russian. Overhead monitors in the Temple itself, and in the classrooms and the outside tent, allowed everyone to see and hear the class in progress.

Each morning had a specific topic:

> Monday — 50-Years of Manifesting the Vision of the Masters, with Jyotish and Devi
>
> Tuesday — Manifesting a Dwapara Way of Life, with Jaya, Shivani, and Asha
>
> Wednesday — Manifesting the Vision Throughout the World, with Ananta, Kirtani, & Dhyana
>
> Thursday — Practical Expressions of the Vision, with Kshama, David Eby, Dharmarajan, Sundara, Zach Abbey, Michelle Dossett, Atman
>
> Friday — Swami Kriyananda and Ananda's Place in World Consciousness, with Dharmadas, Sri Kaarthikeyan, Narya, and Jyotish & Devi

The following is a listing of talks (available online), that I particularly recommend:

> Jyotish and Devi's talks on Monday set the tone for the entire week, welcoming those who were attending and thanking those whose generosity made the Temple of Light possible.
>
> Jaya's talk on Tuesday was clear, impersonal, and broad in vision.

Ananta's talk on Wednesday was exceptional in vision and vibration.

Thursday morning's panel talks I found to be excellent practical applications.

Friday morning's talks were tributes to Swamiji. Each speaker expressed personal experiences with Swamiji in a subtle, touching, and universal way. Throughout was a high level of consciousness that was thrilling to feel.

The evening programs included a Monday evening kirtan, a Tuesday evening showing of *The Answer* movie, and a Wednesday evening performance of scenes from several of Swami's plays (The Land of Golden Sunshine; The Peace Treaty; and Jewel in the Lotus).

Thursday was July 4, the actual fiftieth anniversary of Ananda's founding! It was on this day in 1969 that we purchased the Village property and so launched the first World Brotherhood Colony foreseen by Master. In memory of this auspicious occasion, at 1:45 pm on that day, we held a World Brotherhood Parade. On Master's Market lawn, some twenty-two different nations were represented by Ananda members from around the world: Italy, Spain, England, Hong Kong, Sweden, Croatia, Argentina, Canada, Colombia, Russia, Slovakia, and more.

One by one the representatives of each nation marched toward the stage, singing the country's anthem, holding aloft the flag, and in some cases, wearing the national costume.

What was especially touching to me — and what I felt would have pleased Master and Swami — was that each country was represented in a universal spirit of world brotherhood; through the national identities of the participants shone their deeper reality as devotees on a path of Self-realization.

Thursday evening brought a concert of Swami Kriyananda's music, with choirs and musicians from Ananda worldwide singing and playing his compositions. That evening, as we listened, we deeply felt in Swami's music the universal language of the soul.

Friday's program was an Evening with Swami Kriyananda — a video of our beloved founder, speaking about Ananda and its place in the world.

All day Saturday was the dedication of the Temple of Light.

First came the Invocation of Light: Representatives of the major religions of the world spoke on their chosen way: Christianity, Judaism, Islam, Buddhism, Sikhism, Hinduism, and Self-realization.

(I particularly enjoyed Aditya's talk on the universality of Hinduism.)

Later that day we gathered on The Expanding Light lawn area for a Dedication Dinner, followed by a "Celebrating the Light Procession," moving from The Expanding Light across the meadow to the Temple of Light. Jyotish and Devi and the dignitaries with them stopped in front of the Temple while Pranaba and I continued on with the procession until all of us completely surrounded the Temple. All facing inward toward the Temple, we chanted Aum three times in blessing it; then, facing outward, three more Aums into the world — sending light and blessings from the Temple to all who would come in future, and to all those receptive to the blessings of light emanating from the Temple.

Entering the Sanctuary, we were each given a battery-powered candle. All together we performed an Arati, sending this light out into the world, and ending with our first experience (by the magic of the Temple's lighting system) of this sacred space bathed in blue light.

The next day, Jyotish and Devi gave the first Sunday service in the new Temple.

The service, and the week, concluded with the entire congregation singing Swami's Goodbye song:

Go with love, may joyful blessings

Speed you safely on your way.

May God's light expand within you,

May we be one in that light some day.

After such a profoundly moving week people found it difficult to leave—many lingering on with picture taking and goodbyes and a last meal together.

As the physical Temple was being built, the builders felt that its form, the energy behind it, everything about it was already there—that they were simply tuning in to the vision shared by Swami, Master, Babaji, and all the Masters; the builders were simply drawing that vision out of the ether to make it manifest on the material plane.

There was the feeling too that the completion of this Temple of Light was the beginning of a new phase of Ananda—the beginning of the next fifty years of Master's mission through Ananda.

2019–2022 A Pandemic Is Announced; Ananda Goes Online!

For the next nine months, until March 2020, the Temple of Light was a hub of spiritual activity. We were continually amazed by its beauty, its elegant simplicity, and its functionality. Whenever I walked into the Temple, I thought of the Golden Palace Babaji manifested for Lahiri Mahasaya's initiation into Kriya Yoga. This Temple too, I felt, Babaji had created as his gift to us.

Yogananda's Arrival in Boston: 100-Year Anniversary

The beginning of 2020 saw us preparing for the 100-year anniversary of the arrival in Boston of our guru, Paramhansa Yogananda. Even as a special event in the Boston area was being planned, we were hearing more about a deadly virus spreading rapidly from its point of origin in China. In February we heard of a case in the Bay area, in Vacaville, not far from Ananda Village. Though the news was disturbing its far-reaching implications were not yet apparent to us.

A Final Program at Ananda Portland before the Pandemic (March 6–8, 2020)

Maria McSweeney and I were scheduled to lead a Kriya weekend at the Ananda Church in Portland, Oregon at the beginning of March. As our departure time approached, we watched news reports of the rapid spread of the virus. In the end, we decided to stay with our plan for this retreat, little knowing that we would not travel again for a program such as this for a number of years to come.

We had a good weekend—a Kriya program on Saturday, Sunday Service, and renewed connections with friends on the path. As we were saying goodbye to people after Sunday Service, a friend in the health care business came up to tell us that he felt the impact of this virus would be as deadly as that of the 1918 worldwide flu epidemic. His words came as a shock, but I took them as a good wakeup call about what might lay ahead.

Divine Mother's Hidden Blessings: Ananda's Mission Goes Worldwide Online

March 11, 2020, two days after we flew home from Portland, a worldwide pandemic was declared. I thought immediately of the divine gift of the previous year's gathering of hundreds of our Ananda spiritual family to dedicate the Temple of Light and to celebrate together Ananda's fifty-year anniversary. As the pandemic virus spread and the accompanying lockdowns continued over the next few years, I often called to mind that magical time of our deep connection as a spiritual family.

Coming also to mind was gratitude for Divine Mother's and Babaji's gift to us of the Temple of Light. Specifically designed with high-quality broadcasting equipment the Temple would allow us to stay connected worldwide as a spiritual family during this difficult time. Without the Temple we would have been hard pressed to reach our far-flung Ananda family. How perfectly our gurus had orchestrated the completion of the Temple—truly a transmitting station for God's light in a time of spreading darkness. What a blessing!

Soon after March 11 we began broadcasting videos of hope and inspiration—our weekly Sunday services, now included an additional ten or fifteen-minute video talk specially recorded by the ministers after Sunday service. Outwardly the talks focused on right attitude, simple postures for relaxation, singing and music; inwardly their purpose was to provide people with satsang and a regular connection to Ananda.

We moved quickly to take all our programs online. The Online with Ananda department expanded dramatically in importance. Ananda entered a new era of serving people worldwide. At Ananda Village, The Expanding Light Retreat and the Meditation Retreat were closed; our schools were closed; the entire Village was closed for a time. We waited to see how the pandemic would affect us and the world around us.

Cooperative Spiritual Living in a Time of Crisis

At Ananda Village we worked together helping one another buy necessities such as food and fuel. Because the Village is fifteen miles from town, online ordering greatly expanded. Master's Market, under the guidance of Omprakash, became a focal point, especially for food-related needs. Many of us began having satsang with one another by taking walks around the community—good exercise, good conversation, and a simple way to be together and safely apart at the same time.

Online programs and courses grew apace. For the first time ever, we offered Spiritual Renewal Week entirely online. To our relief (we weren't sure the week would work online) Spiritual Renewal Week was a success—greatly appreciated by all who attended, especially perhaps by the many who for years hadn't been able to attend in person and now were able to do so.

The 100th Anniversary of Yogananda's arrival in Boston was successfully broadcast online in 2020. We were learning as we went how to serve online in this time of great need for spiritual support.

2021 brought a continuance of the pandemic, with only sporadic opportunities for in-person gatherings. The Expanding Light retreat opened and closed several times, then opened again.

As 2022 progressed, we were able to travel as long as we took sensible precautions.

In April 2022, Pranaba and I flew across the country to give a weekend Kriya retreat in Rhode Island; in July we gave programs in Los Angeles.

As the years of the pandemic went by, Ananda not only survived but thrived. As other organizations struggled when they had to close down, our ability to go online with all our classes, services and events kept us financially stable as well as able to continue and even expand our world service.

I worked mainly from home during this time, leading an ongoing study group for a few friends on Zoom.

Blessed Transitions: Seva and Anandi

2021 and 2022 also brought two events of personal significance. Two of my closest spiritual friends passed away unexpectedly. Nayaswami Seva, in November 2021 of a sudden heart attack, and Nayaswami Anandi, after a brief and unexpected illness at the end of January 2022. I had known each of them for over fifty years; we had "grown up" together spiritually—in the Friends of God monastery at Ayodhya in the 1970s, sharing a life of discipleship, guided by Swami Kriyananda as our spiritual teacher.

The day Anandi passed had a special energy. Pranaba and I were scheduled to give the Sunday Service that day in the new Temple of Light. At 8:00 am the entire Village lost power. Though not an unusual event in the foothills, we hadn't lost power right before a Sunday Service in quite a while. Unable to carry on in the Temple without electricity, Pranaba and I, the musicians, and the sound and setup crews, carried what we needed across the meadow and over to the old temple at The Expanding Light. There was a generator there that could power streaming the service online. The one catch was that the generator had only enough power for online transmission, but not enough for also heating the temple. The day was quite cold, but we all bundled up and enjoyed the challenge.

After the service, we returned home and walked down the road to Bharat and Anandi's house. Her body had been moved outside to the garden area—oak trees all around and a beautiful view of the distant mountains. The outside location made it possible for many Village residents, even families with children, to come and sit with her. The setting and the day seemed astral to me, otherworldly; we felt ourselves transported into another realm.

To have both Anandi and Seva gone so quickly was a moment in time for me—I felt both happy and sad at the same time, but the happiness was predominant. I knew each of these close friends to be a deep soul, attuned to Master and Swami; I felt each one would now be living in the joy and grace of God and Guru.

Nayaswami Seva   Nayaswami Anandi

2004, India Pilgrimage
group, Puri

[ABOVE, LEFT] 2004, India, Haridwar Shiva

[ABOVE] 2004, India, Kolkata, Master's Family
Home, 4 Gurpar Road

[LEFT] 2004, India, Kolkata, Master

2004, India Kolkata, Master's Meditation Room

2004, India Ramakrishna, Parvati at the Kalyana Kalpataru (wish-fulfilling tree)

[BELOW] 2004, India Tulsi Bose Home, Pranaba and Parvati

[BELOW, RIGHT] 2004, India Tulsi Bose, Meditation Room

2004, India, Varanasi, boat on the Ganga

2004, India, Varanasi, *arati* on the Ganga

2004, India, Varanasi, laundry on the Ganga

2004, India, Vashishta Guha, entry to the *guha* (cave)

2004, India, Vashishta Guha, the Ganga

2004, India, Vashishta Guha, Parvati meditating

2004, India, Vashishta Guha, Pranaba, Bob, Parvati

2005, India With Swami Kriyananda, *The Essence of the Bhagavad Gita* is finished!

2009, Nayaswami Order Initiation with Nayaswamis Jyotish and Devi, December 24, 2009, The Expanding Light temple

[ABOVE] 2010, Janaka Tea, group with Swami attending

[RIGHT] 2010, Janaka Tea, Parvati speaking

2010, Janaka Tea, Swami enjoying the tea

2010, Janaka Tea, Swami Kriyananda pronam

2010, Janaka Tea, Swami blessing Parvati   2010, Janaka Tea, Swami, Devi, Parvati

2010, Janaka tea, [FROM LEFT] Kent, Lisa, Pranaba, Parvati, Jyoti

[LEFT] 2015, Parvati and Maria, become Kriyacharyas

[BELOW, LEFT] 2015, Parvati SRW

[BELOW] 2017, Parvati SRW

2019, Pavilion of Gratitude, Dedication

[LEFT] 2019, Pavilion of Gratitude, Parvati

[BELOW] 2019, Temple of Light

[ABOVE, LEFT] 2019, Temple of Light, inside, AUM blessing

[ABOVE] 2022, Pranaba and Parvati, at the Crystal Hermitage

Go with Love!

Chapter 6

Paramhansa Yogananda
and Swami Kriyananda

"Thou art my life, Thou art my love,
Thou art the sweetness which I do seek!"

In these lines from *Cosmic Chants* Paramhansa Yogananda describes who God and Guru are to us as seekers. To us at Ananda, Swami Kriyananda made it clear that Paramhansa Yogananda was the guru for those on this path of Self-realization. There was never any question about this. To those of us who were new on the path, Swami explained his own role as spiritual friend and guide. More deeply, Swami was a highly evolved direct disciple of our guru, Paramhansa Yogananda, who was himself an avatar, one who brought a "special dispensation"—a broad spiritual mission—to the West, and to America in particular.

Swami Kriyananda, for his part, brought Yogananda's consciousness to life for us. He helped us understand the guru's role in our spiritual lives and his power to transform us.

Like a superconscious ocean liner, Swami Kriyananda moved through this world sharing the blessings he had received from living with his guru. He was a friend to all, in God. For over forty-two years he blessed my life with Yogananda's consciousness and vibrations. Through Swami Kriyananda, Yogananda has come to me in this lifetime—and I feel to many others. Swami gave me my spiritual life; he supported me both in who I was when I came, and in who I could become spiritually. Always he held the goal before me: God Alone.

I never knew Swami Kriyananda to deviate from his role as divine friend and guide—nor from his essential consciousness. His was a consciousness I felt steadily through the fluctuating circumstances of the years of building Ananda—not only in meditation, but in all the ups and downs of daily life.

I first read *Autobiography of a Yogi* only a few weeks before my first visit to Ananda. I distinctly remember feeling during that visit, "This feels like the Autobiography." At Ananda I found, even in those very early years, the vibration and consciousness I had experienced in Yogananda's book. This was clear proof to me that what was happening at Ananda through Swami Kriyananda and those around him was strongly connected to Yogananda.

Swami Kriyananda was amazing. Not only was he a direct disciple of an avatar; not only was he our spiritual friend and guide; he was also a teacher and lecturer, a writer, editor, singer and song writer, composer, artist, poet, photographer, and "a good cook." Above all he was our friend. He said himself, that he felt he could help people most through simple friendship.

In my early years at Ananda, the years he was building Ananda, I felt his energy as dynamic joy and will power, qualities essential to such an undertaking.

In his later years, this early dynamic energy transformed into an ocean of bliss. I remember sitting in the back of the Yogananda Amphitheater at the Village, during a gathering of some 400 people—I could feel Swami's bliss filling the entire area. Again, at his last public talk in the Bay Area in 2012, his dynamic spiritual energy and bliss filled the whole auditorium. And this at a time when, physically, he couldn't take even one step unaided.

Swami often told us: life is a battlefield. Most people aren't yet aware of this reality; even if they have some awareness, there is little understanding of the nature of the battle. Nor do they realize what the goal is. These truths came into focus for me only when I came on this path and especially when I met Swami Kriyananda. This beginning understanding was my first step as a devotee.

The spiritual path seems long and winding. The difficulty of the journey becomes especially apparent when we realize that the battles we will face lie within ourselves. Swami Kriyananda was always there for those who wanted his support. He helped thousands of truth seekers to continue on the path—giving us solutions, encouragement, joy and love as we continued on. He showed us how we ourselves could find solutions, to keep strong in courage and faith, to feel divine joy and love through our own developing spiritual efforts. I never saw him deviate from his divine service to us all, even unto his last breath.

What this book is about is the story of my life with Ananda and its dynamic success. Paramhansa Yogananda's vibration and consciousness through Swami Kriyananda continues to flow through us as we in turn become channels, sharing the divine gift with "all whom we meet."

Swami Kriyananda, August 2010   Paramhansa Yogananda, March 7, 1952

Chapter 7

Go With Love

The spiritual path is a great adventure—with all the ups and downs that any true adventure has. This one takes place right within your own self, and it has the potential to provide you with the deepest fulfillment imaginable.

My life with Ananda began when I was twenty-five years old. Now more than fifty years later, I find myself still deeply engaged in and fulfilled by the path of Self-realization, graced with the understanding of life given me by my guru, my spiritual teacher, and the practice of Kriya Yoga. Mine has been a direct, living experience, which has seen me through all the highs and lows that have come with the building of Ananda—the death of close friends, a devastating forest fire, a twelve-year lawsuit meant to destroy Ananda, and most recently a worldwide pandemic. Attitudes I have made my own over the years have allowed me to meet each new challenge with inner calmness and a clear focus on how best to move forward—to be solution-oriented and ready to do my part while inwardly knowing that God and guru are with me, guiding my thoughts and actions.

The attitudes and priorities of a spiritual life are different from those of a worldly life. They are not always easy to put into words, but Swami Kriyananda has captured the spirit of them in a children's song:

Life is beautiful, life is gay,

When I give myself away;

When I live to please Thee, Lord,

Dancing in Thy ray.

223

Let me see Thee everywhere,

Hear Thy melodies in the air.

Let me feel Thy strength in me.

Give me joy to share.

As we live more in and from the heart, and make meditation a regular part of our lives, we find the spiritual attitudes expressed in this song becoming natural to us. We find ourselves part of a greater whole, and we experience directly the joy and happiness that come from living more in God's presence.

Eventually, we begin to feel a more personal dimension of the spiritual life, one that is unique to each of us. This is when the soul's call within becomes stronger.

Swami Kriyananda wrote a beautiful song, *God's Call Within*, that speaks of this yearning of the soul.

It begins:

Listen! Listen!

Whispering within your soul:

Hints of laughter, hints of joy;

Sweet songs of sadness, of quenchless yearning

For the Light,

For My love, your true home.

I have found that what provides the energy, inspiration, and commitment to persevere in the spiritual life is love for God, for the Divine Presence at the heart of our own being.

"Perseverance," Swami Kriyananda writes in *The Essence of the Bhagavad Gita*, "is a distinct quality, demanding the continuous re-application of will power to whatever cause one believes is right and worthy. "Perseverance, in its ever-newly creative outlook, is different from stubbornness, which is a refusal to re-examine the facts, or to reappraise one's position with regard to them. Perseverance means not to allow oneself to be dissuaded or diverted from one's worthwhile goals, but to meet every difficulty creatively, with new solutions, until one's ends have been achieved.

"Thus, perseverance means to be willing to re-examine one's position and, if necessary, to correct one's first assumptions, thereafter seeking ever-new avenues by which a worthwhile goal may be achieved. It means to be firm in the faith that what is right and true *must*, eventually, come to pass, provided one holds firmly to high principle."

It is this understanding of perseverance that has allowed so many of my gurubhais, myself included, to continue on the spiritual path for many years. It has been perseverance that has built Ananda.

And the goal of the spiritual path? Self-realization. Paramhansa Yogananda's definition is a wonderfully open and inviting call to begin a spiritual journey that brings joy and complete fulfillment:

"Self-realization is the knowing in all parts of body, mind,
and soul that you are now in possession of the kingdom of
God; that you do not have to pray that it come to you; that
God's omnipresence is your omnipresence; and that all that
you need to do is improve your knowing."

To "improve your knowing" is what each one of us is given to do in order to live a deepening spiritual life—one day at a time, applying yourself with love, courage, and strength to the best of your ability to the teachings and techniques given to you by God and guru.

Paramhansa Yogananda said, "You have to live anyway. Why not live in the right way?"

Why not indeed! You will never regret the effort you make.

I leave you now with the Ananda *Goodbye Song*, written by Swami Kriyananda, which beautifully expresses the wish we have for one another as we move ever closer to our oneness in Him:

Go with love. May joyful blessings

Speed you safely on your way.

May God's light expand within you.

May we be one in that light someday.

2005, With Swami Kriyananda in India

Acknowledgements

SWAMI KRIYANANDA

I have felt inspired, and almost compelled, to write about my life with Ananda in order to express my deepest gratitude to Swami Kriyananda. His ongoing support, love, and joy have given me a life worth living, full of meaning and joy. Through his dedicated attunement to his guru, Paramhansa Yogananda, Swami Kriyananda has brought outward expression to the way of life that Yogananda described when he spoke of "World Brotherhood Communities." Ananda is dedicated to the ongoing fulfillment of Yogananda's mission to the world in this extraordinary time in this world's evolution.

NAYASWAMI PRAKASH

I would also like to thank Nayaswami Prakash. This book would not have been possible without his dedicated editing of the manuscript. I learned a lot about the English language by working with him for the year that it took to edit it. Prakash also lived through the early years of Ananda, and was able to help me put into words the feeling of that time.

NAYASWAMI PRANABA

My husband, partner, and supporter in the many adventures we have lived through with Ananda and Swami Kriyananda. Pranaba's ongoing support, understanding, encouragement and love have made this book possible.

BARBARA BINGHAM, PHOTOGRAPHER, GURUBHAI

Barbara has helped make possible the inclusion of many of the photos found in this book. These photos help bring to life things about my life with Ananda that are not easily put into words.

About Paramhansa Yogananda

 Born in 1893, Paramhansa Yogananda was the first yoga master of India to take up permanent residence in the West.

He arrived in America in 1920 and traveled throughout the country on what he called his "spiritual campaigns." Hundreds of thousands filled the largest halls in major cities to see the yoga master from India. Yogananda continued to lecture and write up to his passing in 1952.

Yogananda's initial impact on Western culture was truly impressive. His lasting spiritual legacy has been even greater. His *Autobiography of a Yogi*, first published in 1946, helped launch a spiritual revolution in the West. Translated into more than fifty languages, it remains a best-selling spiritual classic to this day.

Before embarking on his mission, Yogananda received this admonition from his teacher, Swami Sri Yukteswar: "The West is high in material attainments but lacking in spiritual understanding. It is God's will that you play a role in teaching mankind the value of balancing the material with an inner, spiritual life."

In addition to *Autobiography of a Yogi*, Yogananda's spiritual legacy includes music, poetry, and extensive commentaries on the Bhagavad Gita, the Rubaiyat of Omar Khayyam, and the Christian Bible, showing the principles of Self-realization as the unifying truth underlying all true religions. Through his teachings and his Kriya Yoga path millions of people around the world have found a new way to connect personally with God.

His mission, however, was far broader than all this. It was to help usher the whole world into Dwapara Yuga, the new Age of Energy in which we live. "Someday," Swami Kriyananda wrote, "I believe he will be seen as the *avatar* of Dwapara Yuga: the way shower for a new age."

About Swami Kriyananda

 A prolific author, accomplished composer, playwright, and artist, and a world-renowned spiritual teacher, Swami Kriyananda (1926–2013) referred to himself simply as a close disciple of the great God-realized master, Paramhansa Yogananda. He met his guru at the age of twenty-two, and served him during the last four years of the Master's life. He dedicated the rest of his life to sharing Yogananda's teachings throughout the world.

Kriyananda was born in Romania of American parents, and educated in Europe, England, and the United States. Philosophically and artistically inclined from youth, he soon came to question life's meaning and society's values. During a period of intense inward reflection, he discovered Yogananda's *Autobiography of a Yogi*, and immediately traveled three thousand miles from New York to California to meet the Master, who accepted him as a monastic disciple. Yogananda appointed him as the head of the monastery, authorized him to teach and give Kriya initiation in his name, and entrusted him with the missions of writing, teaching, and creating what he called "world brotherhood colonies."

Kriyananda founded the first such community, Ananda Village, in the Sierra Nevada foothills of Northern California in 1968. Ananda is recognized as one of the most successful intentional communities in the world today. It has served as a model for other such communities that he founded subsequently in the United States, Europe, and India.

About the Author

Nayaswami Parvati is one of the founding members of Ananda, and is one of Ananda's most widely traveled and experienced ministers. She moved to Ananda in 1972, and was made a minister by Swami Kriyananda in 1981. With her husband, Pranaba, she has been involved in the creation and direction of Ananda centers and communities in Palo Alto, Portland, Seattle, Dallas, and Assisi, Italy. Parvati has served as the Executive Director of the Ananda Janaka Foundation since March 2004.

FURTHER EXPLORATIONS

CRYSTAL CLARITY PUBLISHERS

If you enjoyed this title, Crystal Clarity Publishers invites you to deepen your spiritual life through many additional resources based on the teachings of Paramhansa Yogananda. We offer books, e-books, audiobooks, yoga and meditation videos, and a wide variety of inspirational and relaxation music composed by Swami Kriyananda.

See a listing of books below, visit our secure website for a complete online catalog, or place an order for our products.

crystalclarity.com

800.424.1055 | **clarity@crystalclarity.com**

1123 Goodrich Blvd. | Commerce, CA 90022

ANANDA WORLDWIDE

Crystal Clarity Publishers is the publishing house of Ananda, a worldwide spiritual movement founded by Swami Kriyananda, a direct disciple of Paramhansa Yogananda. Ananda offers resources and support for your spiritual journey through meditation instruction, webinars, online virtual community, email, and chat.

Ananda has centers and meditation groups in over 45 countries, offering group guided meditations, classes and teacher training in meditation and yoga, and many other resources.

In addition, Ananda has residential communities in the US, Europe, and India. Spiritual communities are places where people live together in a spirit of cooperation and friendship, dedicated to a common goal. Spirituality is practiced in all areas of daily life: at school, at work, or in the home. Many Ananda communities offer internships during which one can stay and experience spiritual community firsthand.

For more information about Ananda communities or meditation groups near you, please visit **ananda.org** or call 530.478.7560.

THE EXPANDING LIGHT RETREAT

The Expanding Light is the largest retreat center in the world to share exclusively the teachings of Paramhansa Yogananda. Situated in the Ananda Village community near Nevada City, California, the center offers the opportunity to experience spiritual life in a contemporary ashram setting. The varied, year-round schedule of classes and programs on yoga, meditation, and spiritual practice includes Karma Yoga, personal retreat, spiritual travel, and online learning. Large groups are welcome.

The Ananda School of Yoga & Meditation offers certified yoga, yoga therapist, spiritual counselor, and meditation teacher trainings.

The teaching staff has years of experience practicing Kriya Yoga meditation and all aspects of Paramhansa Yogananda's teachings. You may come for a relaxed personal renewal, participating in ongoing activities as much or as little as you wish. The serene mountain setting, supportive staff, and delicious vegetarian meals provide an ideal environment for a truly meaningful stay, be it a brief respite or an extended spiritual vacation.

For more information, please visit **expandinglight.org** or call 800.346.5350.

ANANDA MEDITATION RETREAT

Set amidst seventy-two acres of beautiful meditation gardens and wild forest in Northern California's Sierra foothills, the Ananda Meditation Retreat is an ideal setting for a rejuvenating, inner experience.

The Meditation Retreat has been a place of deep meditation and sincere devotion for over fifty years. Long before that, the Native American Maidu tribe held this to be sacred land. The beauty and presence of the Divine are tangibly felt by all who visit here.

Studies show that being in nature and using techniques such as forest bathing can significantly reduce stress and blood pressure while strengthening your immune system, concentration, and level of happiness. The Meditation Retreat is the perfect place for quiet immersion in nature.

Plan a personal retreat, enjoy one of the guided retreats, or choose from a variety of programs led by the caring and joyful staff.

For more information or to place your reservation, please visit **meditationretreat.org**, email **meditationretreat@ananda.org**, or call 530.478.7557.

The Originals Writings of Paramhansa Yogananda

Yogananda's Spiritual Masterpiece
The Original 1946 Unedited Edition

AUTOBIOGRAPHY OF A YOGI
Paramhansa Yogananda

Autobiography of a Yogi is one of the world's most acclaimed spiritual classics, with millions of copies sold. Named one of the Best 100 Spiritual Books of the twentieth century, this book helped launch and continues to inspire a spiritual awakening throughout the Western world.

Yogananda was the first yoga master of India whose mission brought him to settle and teach in the West. His firsthand account of his life experiences in India includes childhood revelations, stories of his visits to saints and masters, and long-secret teachings of yoga and Self-realization that he first made available to the Western reader.

This reprint of the original 1946 edition is free from textual changes made after Yogananda's passing in 1952. This updated edition includes bonus materials: the last chapter that Yogananda wrote in 1951, also without posthumous changes, the eulogy Yogananda wrote for Gandhi, and a new foreword and afterword by Swami Kriyananda, one of Yogananda's close, direct disciples.

Also available in Spanish and Hindi from Crystal Clarity Publishers.

SCIENTIFIC HEALING AFFIRMATIONS
Paramhansa Yogananda

Yogananda's 1924 classic, reprinted here, is a pioneering work in the fields of self-healing and self-transformation. He explains that words are crystallized thoughts and have life-changing power when spoken with conviction, concentration, willpower, and feeling. Yogananda offers far more than mere suggestions for achieving positive attitudes. He shows how to impregnate words with spiritual force to shift habitual thought patterns of the mind and create a new personal reality.

Added to this text are over fifty of Yogananda's well-loved "Short Affirmations," taken from issues of *East-West* and *Inner Culture* magazines from 1932 to 1942. This little book will be a treasured companion on the road to realizing your highest, divine potential.

METAPHYSICAL MEDITATIONS
Paramhansa Yogananda

Metaphysical Meditations is a classic collection of meditation techniques, visualizations, affirmations, and prayers from the great yoga master, Paramhansa Yogananda. The meditations given are of three types: those spoken to the individual consciousness, prayers or demands addressed to God, and affirmations that bring us closer to the Divine.

Select a passage that meets your specific need and speak each word slowly and purposefully until you become absorbed in its inner meaning. At the bedside, by the meditation seat, or while traveling—one can choose no better companion than this.

SONGS OF THE SOUL
Paramhansa Yogananda

Yogananda preferred to express his wisdom not in dry intellectual terms but as pure, expansive feeling. To drink his poetry is to be drawn into the web of his boundless, childlike love. In one moment his *Songs of the Soul* invite us to join him as he plays among the stars with his Cosmic Beloved. Then they call us to discover that portion of our own hearts that is eternally one with the Nearest and Dearest. This volume is a bubbling, singing wellspring of spiritual healing that we can bring with us everywhere.

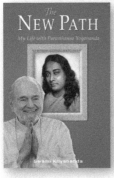

THE NEW PATH
My Life with Paramhansa Yogananda
Swami Kriyananda

Winner of the 2010 Eric Hoffer Award for Best Self-Help/Spiritual Book
Winner of the 2010 USA Book News Award for Best Spiritual Book

The New Path is a moving revelation of one man's search for lasting happiness. After rejecting the false promises offered by modern society, J. Donald Walters found himself (much to his surprise) at the feet of Paramhansa Yogananda, asking to become his disciple. How he got there, trained with the Master, and became Swami Kriyananda makes fascinating reading.

The rest of the book is the fullest account by far of what it was like to live with and be a disciple of that great man of God.

Anyone hungering to learn more about Yogananda will delight in the hundreds of stories of life with a great avatar and the profound lessons they offer. This book is an ideal complement to *Autobiography of a Yogi.*

PARAMHANSA YOGANANDA
A Biography with Personal Reflections and Reminiscences
Swami Kriyananda

Paramhansa Yogananda's life was filled with astonishing accomplishments. And yet in his classic autobiography, he wrote more about the saints he'd met than about his own spiritual attainments. Yogananda's direct disciple, Swami Kriyananda, relates the untold story of this great master and world teacher: his teenage miracles, his challenges in coming to America, his national lecture campaigns, his struggles to fulfill his world-changing mission amid incomprehension and painful betrayals, and his ultimate triumphant achievement.

Kriyananda's subtle grasp of his guru's inner nature and outward mission reveals Yogananda's many-sided greatness. Includes many never-before-published anecdotes and an insider's view of the Master's last years.

TRAINED IN DIVINE LOVE
My Life with Paramhanda Yogananda and Swami Kriyananda
Nayaswami Anandi

For fifty years, Nayaswami Anandi was a deeply devoted disciple of Paramhansa Yogananda, and a student of his beloved disciple, Swami Kriyananda. To everyone she met, Anandi was a beautiful channel of divine love; her life's quest was to reciprocate and express the pure love she received.

In this book, there are sacred and precious experiences and stories never shared before by Anandi. She shares stories about her journey on the Spiritual Path, guidance from Swami Kriyananda, and personal correspondence with Yogananda which capture the intimate dialogue that develops between devoted disciple and guru.

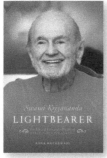

SWAMI KRIYANANDA, LIGHTBEARER
The Life and Legacy of a disciple of Paramhansa Yogananda
by Asha Nayaswami

Kriyananda's life was a triumphant life, but not an easy one, tested as he was by ill-health, financial challenges, and years of bitter estrangement from fellow disciples. His life story is told in the struggle as well as the victory. A great soul incarnates to awaken faith in our own spiritual potential. Asha writes, "A great wave of Divine Light is sweeping over the planet. If you tune in to that Light, you, too, will become an instrument of that Light."

This firsthand account of life with Swami Kriyananda is more than a biography. It is a guidebook for spiritual living, showing us a path of light that all may follow. And it is a labor of love by Asha that was forty-four years in the making.

FAITH IS MY ARMOR
The Life of Swami Kriyananda
by Nayaswami Devi Novak

This is the story of a man who achieved extraordinary victories in his life—not with weapons, but with moral and spiritual courage. The life of Swami Kriyananda is the story of a man who has, to an amazing degree, demonstrated spiritual courage, determination in the face of great obstacles, and personal sacrifice for an ideal.

Faith Is My Armor tells the complete story of his life: from his childhood in Rumania, to his desperate search for meaning in life, and to his training under his great Guru, the Indian Master, Paramhansa Yogananda. As a youth of 22, he first met and pledged his discipleship to Yogananda, entering the monastery Yogananda had founded in Southern California.

In the over sixty years since then, Swami Kriyananda traveled and lived around the world, lecturing in five languages, wrote over 100 books and 400 pieces of music, and founded seven spiritual communities in the United States, Europe, and India.

It also recounts the drama of the powerful opposition and attacks he faced as he strove to fulfill the mission his Guru had bestowed upon him.

This book will bring inspiration and hope to all who read it, and renewed faith in the power of God in our lives.

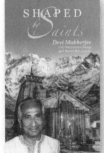

SHAPED BY SAINTS
Devi Mukherjee

While a young man, Devi Mukherjee worked with Mahatma Gandhi in the Indian resistance movement and was imprisoned for five months. After release, Devi began a spiritual quest throughout India, traveling for some forty-five years at various times.

From 1955–1966 he was part of the Yogoda Satsanga Society, Yogananda's organization in India. There, he and Swami Kriyananda were brother monks. He later married the daughter of Yogananda's childhood friend Tulsi Bose. The Mukherjee family lived in Tulsi's former house in Calcutta where he and Yogananda dreamed and meditated as boys.

Devi takes the reader on a deeply inspiring pilgrimage to meet saints and realized masters of modern India in forest ashrams, mountain caves, holy places, and shrines. He shares many insights and lessons from the great ones and tells many previously unpublished stories of Yogananda's early life and return visit to India in 1935–36.

THANK YOU, MASTER
Direct Disciples Remember Paramhansa Yogananda
Hare Krishna Ghosh, Meera Ghosh, Peggy Deitz

Anyone who has read and loved *Autobiography of a Yogi* will be delighted to find this treasure of personal experiences and heartfelt remembrances of Paramhansa Yogananda by three of his direct disciples.

Stories from Yogananda's family members, Hare Krishna Ghosh and Meera Ghosh, who became disciples as teenagers, take the reader on pilgrimage to India to the sacred places and miraculous moments shared with this great yogi. The stories of Peggy Deitz transport one to Yogananda's ashram in California and his life with devotees in America.

Whether humorous or miraculous, mundane or divine, these stories bring to life the experience of being in Yogananda's presence. They give insight into the profound love with which he guided each individual.

Firsthand accounts from close disciples are a gift that helps us tune in to his vast nature. These delightful stories will touch your heart and uplift your spirit.

SWAMIJI
Swami Kriyananda's Last Years; Lessons Learned by His Nurse
by Miriam Rodgers

Paramhansa Yogananda once said to a group of disciples: "You must not let the symphony of your life go unfinished."

This phrase perfectly describes the last years of Swami Kriyananda's life, which were a crescendo of divine love and untiring service to humanity.

In this profoundly moving biographical account filled with never before heard stories, you'll glimpse the interior castle of Swami Kriyananda's consciousness. Rodgers shares an intimate and up-close look at lessons she learned through her connection as Swami Kriyananda's nurse for the last fourteen years of his life.

Throughout history, the saints alone are the true custodians of religion. Saints like Swami Kriyananda draw their understanding from the direct experience of truth and of God, not from superficial reasoning or book learning.

MY HEART REMEMBERS SWAMI KRIYANANDA
Narayani Anaya

Narayani was twenty-four when she first met Swami Kriyananda in 2003. He was seventy-seven, a global teacher and foremost disciple of Paramhansa Yogananda. Recognition was immediate. Her heart declared, "My King!" He said, "She seems like a daughter to me."

Soon she began following Swami around the world—India, America, Europe. In 2010 he asked her to become his personal assistant and caregiver. Since that day on, and literally, until his last breath, Narayani was always by his side. Decades of spiritual training were compressed into a few short years, preparing her to carry his spirit and message of Self-realization to her generation of seekers, and to all who would know God.

THE NEED FOR SPIRITUAL COMMUNITIES AND HOW TO START THEM
Swami Kriyananda

In this book Swami Kriyananda shares the wisdom gained through many decades of study and practice of the principles that make modern communities thrive. Inspired by his guru, Paramhansa Yogananda, and his ideal of "world brotherhood colonies," Kriyananda brought these principles to fruition through persistent effort and inspired leadership.

Kriyananda (1926–2013) founded nine spiritual communities in the United States, Europe, and India and have been hailed as the most successful in the world. These communities were formed on two basic principles: "people are more important than things" and "where there is right action, there is victory." Adherence to these principles is one of the secrets to Ananda's success.

Whether you are interested in communities from a philosophical perspective or from a practical one—and wish to form your own or join with others in doing so—this book will bring you hundreds of helpful insights into the process—how to start a community, how to make it prosper even in difficult times, and how to see it continue into a bright future.